COME DINE WITH ME

COME DINE WITH ME

Special Occasions

Books

TRANSWORLD PUBLISHERS
61–63 Uxbridge Road, London W5 5SA
A Random House Group Company
www.rbooks.co.uk

First published in Great Britain in 2011 by Channel 4 Books
an imprint of Transworld Publishers

Recipe editor: Jeni Wright
Photography: Dan Jones
Food stylist: Emma Marsden

The recipes in this book are based upon those submitted by the enthusiastic
amateur winners of the *Come Dine With Me* television series.

Come Dine With Me is made by ITV Studios for Channel 4 Television.

A CIP catalogue record for this book is available from the British Library.

ISBN 9781905026791

Addresses for Random House Group Ltd companies outside the UK can be found at:
www.randomhouse.co.uk

The Random House Group Ltd Reg. No. 954009

The Random House Group Limited supports The Forest Stewardship Council (FSC),
the leading international forest-certification organization. All our titles that are
printed on Greenpeace-approved FSC-certified paper carry the FSC logo. Our paper
procurement policy can be found at www.rbooks.co.uk/environment

Designed by Smith & Gilmour, London
Typeset in Bliss
Printed and bound in Italy

2 4 6 8 10 9 7 5 3 1

contents

introduction

Welcome to the second volume of *Come Dine With Me*. Two years on from the first cookbook, the TV programme continues to go from strength to strength and it now features more adventurous food than ever before. To reflect this, book two is packed full of handy hints and tips on how to entertain on those extra-special occasions. From Christmas feasts to big summer parties the whole entertaining year is covered, and there is also a guide to throwing your own *Come Dine With Me* evening, a trend that's becoming more and more popular across the nation. There are useful guides on when different produce is in season, so you can make the most of classic ingredients when they are at their very best. And, of course, there are a sprinkling of new anecdotes on the fantastic highs and hysterical lows experienced by our on-screen competitors.

The book also brings together the very best of the recipes created by the contestants and cooked by them on the show. Many of the dishes helped their creators to victory, while the remainder are the best of the rest as chosen by the *Come Dine With Me* team. Some of the recipes have been used in their entirety, while others have been tested and then edited and/or simplified for the everyday cook. All are based on the inspirational ideas of our talented contestants, and there are plenty of options for meat-eaters, pescatarians and vegetarians alike.

So whatever time of year you're entertaining, and however varied your guest list, this book will help you make sure you get your dinner party celebration just right.

spring

The dark nights have finally disappeared. Spring is in the air, and there's new produce in the shops. And if you're an advocate of seasonal eating, you can kiss goodbye to a diet heavily reliant on root vegetables and welcome back greens. This is the time of year when you can start to think differently about entertaining — the variable British climate means that you can get balmier days in April than August, so there are lots of potential opportunities to entertain. However, keep your plans flexible right up to the last minute, to make the most of unexpected spring sunshine.

The big entertaining event is the Easter weekend, but don't forget that it's also Mother's Day and, if you're really into your regional entertaining (or like any excuse for a dinner party), saints' days for England, Ireland and Wales.

Here are a few of the foods that are in season at this time of the year (foods without specific months in brackets are available throughout the entire season).

Vegetables
Asparagus (April/May)
Carrots
Cauliflower
Jersey new potatoes (April/May)
Kale (till end of April)
Leeks (till end of April)
Lettuce (April/May)
Mushrooms
Radish (late April/early May)
Rhubarb (April/May)
Savoy cabbage (March)
Spinach (late April/early May)
Spring greens (till end of April)
Watercress (late April/early May)

Meat
Hare
Lamb
Pigeon
Rabbit

Fish
Crab
Haddock (April/May)
Halibut (March)
Lobster (April/May)
Mackerel (March)
Prawns
Salmon (April)
Trout (April/May)

mother's day

Breakfast in bed is special, but that shouldn't be the beginning and end of treating your mum – it is, after all, Mother's Day and not Mother's Breakfast Bit of the Day.

Be sure to go the extra mile. Obviously that could mean going out to lunch, but didn't you do that last year, and the year before that, too? And don't you go out quite a lot as a family? If so, why not enjoy a home-cooked lunch at home for once? Your mum will probably be really touched that you've done more than ring her favourite restaurant that's on speed-dial.

Plus, she probably slaves over a hot stove for most of the year, so this is the one day every year when you can ban her from her own kitchen. There is no excuse to allow her in, even if she does think dad can burn salad and that you struggle to open a tin of beans. Or she's worried about her pots and pans. Or she doesn't want her prize knife ruined. None of it is an excuse. Shove a gin and tonic, or a sherry (or a mojito if she's that kind of girl), into her hand and coax her to put her feet up whilst you cause carnage in her kitchen.

Better still, make it all a surprise. Obviously if you no longer live at home then it's easy: make an arrangement like, 'Come round at noon and we'll go to a restaurant from there.' Then when she arrives, everyone's waiting for her, complete with a glass of her favourite tipple and the food on the go.

Or maybe you're the dad, your kids still live at home, and it's your other half you've got to spoil. If this is the case and you're in charge of the cooking, things can be a bit trickier. There's only one thing for it: use the kids as a decoy to get her out of the house for a while – after all, it is mainly their job to treat her. Buy her a decadent treatment at a local spa, or a hot chocolate at a local café might do the trick. Promise that it will be followed by lunch out, and then surprise her back at home. Make sure that the plan for the day gives you a good excuse for staying behind.

Once she's out of the house with the kids, it's down to you to sort the cooking, the drinks and the décor – the full works. Allow at least a couple of hours. Then the kids need a plausible reason to come back to the house en route to lunch. Maybe pick a restaurant which you all have to drive to together, so that they have to bring her back home to collect the car (and you).

Now for the tricky part: what you are going to cook. If your other half is the one who does most of the cooking and she's always asking other people what they'd like, then you may not be certain of her favourite meals. Try to do some crafty research, but investigate a good way in advance of the day itself to ensure that she doesn't become suspicious.

Whatever you choose, try to pick a starter and a dessert which you can prepare beforehand, and a main that can be popped into the oven before she gets back so that you don't get stuck in the kitchen – that way everyone can enjoy a proper family meal together. For a real touch of class, add some canapés, since they're easy but really delicious. Remember that you might not have lots of cooking time, because even the best decoy plan might not leave you hours and hours to prepare.

Next, if you're not a great cook but you want to create a truly memorable dining experience, practise the meal. There's just one small problem: where to do it. There are two options: pretend to play football/tennis/golf or be stuck at work/in a traffic jam (delete as appropriate) then nip round to a friend's house to test out the meal. Once again keep the excuse plausible – if the last time you kicked a football was sometime at the end of the twentieth century then you might find yourself with a very suspicious spouse on your hands. Also bear in mind that practising on away turf – with different pots and cookers – isn't going to ensure it will all run smoothly on the big day itself so factor that in, otherwise it could all go horribly wrong.

Make the most of opportunities to practise on home turf when your partner is out and you've got the house to yourself. Cooking is like everything else – you get better with practice. If every time it tastes like something you wouldn't even feed to the dog, try something else. Plus, remember to clean up scrupulously afterwards so as not to arouse suspicion.

The run-up to Mother's Day: So you've set the menu and perfected it. Now it's all down to the preparation for the big day.

Two weeks before (if not more): Go shopping for a present, something that's a real treat. Snoop around to see if she's run out of her favourite perfume. It's the start of a new season, so perhaps something to brighten her wardrobe would do the trick. Don't leave the present to the last minute – there's more than enough to do with lunch to sort out.

A week before: After the dry run, timetable the big day. Don't assume that mum will be straight out of the house at the crack of dawn so that you have plenty of time. It's her day and she'll want to do things leisurely, so always work on the worst-case scenario that you could have as little as an hour alone in the house. If you want to buy her flowers, order a delivery since you probably won't have time to go out and pick them up.

A couple of days before: You could go shopping on the day itself, but if you're going to struggle to get your other half out of the house then you don't want to waste valuable time at the supermarket. Plus it's a Sunday, so the shops won't open till 10am at the earliest, probably even 11am. Buy the ingredients a few days in advance, then ask a favour from a neighbour and see if they can look after them for you (just keep your fingers crossed that they don't develop a penchant for salmon roulade). You could of course try to hide the food at home, but most women will spot an alien object in their fridge so you'll be rumbled. Whatever you do, don't forget the booze.

The day: Try to stick to your timetable, but if you start falling behind then at least make sure that the starter's done and the table's laid by the time the family returns – most women love a well-laid table, especially if there are flowers at the centre. Make sure that one of the kids gives you good notice of their return – a phone call perhaps, telling you what time they'll be back. Have a glass of something decadent at the ready, plus the flowers for the moment she walks through the door. And don't forget those canapés, if you've had time. Finally let lunch be served – hopefully to perfection because it's so well practised!

easter

The break from Good Friday to Easter Monday is a time for family and friends to get together and entertain, but that doesn't mean you have to replicate the Christmas food-fest/nightmare-cooking marathon.

Vary your entertaining over the long weekend: Good Friday or Easter Saturday could be the time for a proper dinner party, when you can use the long weekend to catch up with friends; Easter Sunday could be the perfect day for a family lunch; and Easter Monday could be all about a high tea after a long walk in the fresh spring air.

There's also the option of brunch if your mates are the sorts who see any bank holiday as a reason to go out on the town – they'll probably appreciate nothing more than a hearty midday meal after crawling out of bed barely an hour earlier.

Food: As for what to cook, tradition says that Easter is all about lamb, plus of course fish on a Friday. Don't box yourself in with that, though – instead use newly available springtime ingredients. Be flexible with your menu planning, since it's that time of year when the weather is at its changeable worst. If you set your heart on a barbeque it will be pouring with rain; plan to cook up a roast with all the trimmings and it will be baking outside and everyone will be dying to enjoy their first taste of sunshine for months (whilst you sweat away in the kitchen).

Draw up a range of menus to cope with the variety of different weathers which might be thrown at you – and the chances are, knowing the vagaries of the British climate, you could even use all of them across the course of one weekend. The list should include everything from a hearty sit-down meal that'll warm the cockles to a lighter lunch in keeping with a spring day, and perhaps even the full alfresco dining experience, complete with barbeque (see more on barbies later, pages 47 to 50).

If you are going for the hearty sit-down meal, don't forget to make the most of vegetables which are in season. Say no to those wintery roots, as people will have had enough of munching through squash, parsnip and sweet potato for the last three months. Your party needs to have the fresh air of spring, rather than the stale air of winter. For the same reason steer clear of turkey and goose because that smacks of a re-run of Christmas (and everyone's still probably trying to shift that last annoying half pound of winter flab and they don't need a reminder of their festive over-eating).

Once you've planned your different menu options, leave shopping to the last possible moment and get hold of the best weather forecast you can. If there's any hint of rain, play it safe and avoid the outdoor barbeque option.

With the obligatory Easter egg hunt to plan, plus other games to organize, it also helps to prepare in the morning – so ditch the risotto and think of dishes which can be prepared in advance, such as Moroccan lamb (page 31), roast fillet of beef (page 32) or roast marmalade chicken (page 28).

Then there's the question of pudding. Whatever you do, don't use the Easter egg hunt as a replacement. Why, I hear you ask? Simple, there will always be some among the children (or even the grown-ups) who love nothing more than hoarding their eggs. They eat one a day. They savour each one by enjoying it for as long as possible. Then they rub their brother or sister's nose in it because their sibling has already guzzled theirs. Make find-your-own-chocolate a replacement pudding and you'll have some disappointed kids on your hands ...

Choose something light and nothing with lots of last-minute cooking or elaborate assembly. Zesty flavours are great, but you could of course use Easter Sunday as an excuse to naughtily incorporate some chocolate into your dessert.

Entertainment: Easter is smack in the middle of the school holidays so there may be children around – which probably means a lunch option on at least one day, with entertainment before or after.

For a classic Easter egg hunt it's pretty obvious what you need – chocolate eggs. But to enjoy the hunt to the full, and to get some hearty fresh air and exercise (or to wear out the kids), you also need a good open space to hide them in, so it quickly becomes clear which member of the family, or which friend, will be hosting.`

After that it is fairly simple, bar one thing: remembering where you've hidden all the eggs. With so much catering for a family or friends' lunch to do, it's all too easy to distribute the chocolate treasure without memorizing where it's all gone. The kids will be desperate to know how many sweet treats they're looking for, and if they find 90 per cent of them but can't locate the final few you can brace yourself for temper tantrums.

As ever it's worth having a wet-weather option up your sleeve, so when planning the hunt for your garden, create a similar plan for indoors. There are endless nooks and crannies where eggs can be hidden, and you can make it even more like a treasure hunt with clues to guide the searchers to the chocolate.

There is a school of thought that says that once the kids have started in the garden (and after they've enjoyed a good lunch) they'll still probably have lots of energy to burn off, so you should continue the games. Lay on an egg-and-spoon race, or a three-legged race. You name it, get them to do it.

Don't spare the grown-ups. After all, there's nothing better for tired kids than seeing their parents make fools of themselves – it's guaranteed to perk up their flagging spirits. Feel free to be sadistic and make the adults compete in all the trickiest races you can think of. It can also be subtle revenge on those guests who've been over-imbibing while you've been playing the super-duper party organizer.

To help plan your weekend, here's a quick guide to the key things to do – and when.

Two weeks before: Plan your different menu options.

Four days before: Buy the chocolate and anything else you need for your fun and games, if that's your choice. Make a clear note of how many eggs you'll be hiding.

Three days before: Prepare little baskets for the kids to carry away their hoards of eggs. Feel free to buy the baskets, but it's nice to add a little personal touch with a ribbon and name tag – plus that way there can be no confusion on departure when the greedy kids attempt to steal more than their fair share!

Two days before: Check the weather forecast, decide on your final menu and shop for it.

One day before: Take any meats which need defrosting out of the freezer. Make jellies for trifles, or other things that need time to set. Set and decorate the table. If you are using one of those mad dinner-party-planning guides which suggest doing things like buying stick-on letters and writing everyone's names on boiled eggs, using stuffed bunnies as centrepieces and buying yellow napkins to match the daffodils, don't. Life is too short.

However, don't ignore the table decorations completely: add that extra little touch with some seasonal flowers. Whatever you choose, take extra care with them, and don't forget hay-fever sufferers. If they're picked from your own garden, you don't want to suffer the same fate as *Come Dine With Me* contestant Nigel Beaumont from Bradford, who picked laburnum for his table only for one of his diners to claim it is poisonous and then spot greenfly on the table. (Luckily, nothing or no one was poisoned, except for the atmosphere!)

On the day: Do as much meal preparation as possible before everyone descends. Check your chocolate egg supply, just in case cheeky little fingers have been secretly dipping into your stash. Finally, have fun concocting a complicated Easter egg hunt to keep the kids quiet for the whole afternoon …

canapés, amuse-bouches & starters

Andrew Lloyd

spicy & sour prawn soup

1.2 litres fish stock
5cm piece galangal, finely chopped
1 stalk lemongrass, pounded
   and halved crossways
8 kaffir lime leaves (fresh or frozen)
16 baby button mushrooms, halved
   or quartered depending on size
1–2 red chillies, finely chopped (with
   or without seeds according to taste)
juice of 2 limes
large handful of fresh coriander leaves,
   roughly chopped
12 uncooked tiger prawns, peeled
   and deveined

SERVES FOUR

This is my favourite Thai starter and really authentic. The sourness and the spiciness really do shine through, and you can taste every element. It's so easy to make and great fun too. Don't forget to remove the lemongrass, galangal and lime leaves before serving the soup to the guests – I think I got marked down because I left a piece of galangal in one of the bowls!

1 Pour the stock into a large saucepan and bring to the boil. Drop in the galangal, lemongrass, lime leaves and mushrooms. Cover and simmer gently for 15 minutes.

2 Meanwhile, divide the chillies, lime juice and coriander between 4 warmed bowls.

3 Add the prawns to the stock and cook for 1–2 minutes only, just until they turn pink. Remove from the heat and discard the galangal, lemongrass and lime leaves.

4 Ladle the soup into 4 warmed bowls and serve at once.

Eliano Amato

basil tagliatelle with prawn & salmon sauce

300g '00' flour, or 150g plain flour
   and 150g bread flour
1 tsp dried basil
1 large pinch of salt
3 large eggs
1 large egg yolk
2 tbsp olive oil
4 tbsp finely chopped fresh basil
basil sprigs, to garnish

FOR THE SAUCE
200g skinless salmon fillet
400ml whole milk
50g butter
2 tbsp plain flour
1 tbsp salt
4 tbsp freshly grated Parmesan or
   Grana Padano cheese
1 tbsp chopped fresh flat-leaf parsley
½ tsp garlic granules or crushed garlic
150g shelled cooked prawns

SERVES FOUR

This is easier than you think and makes it look like you have gone to a lot of trouble. It is a dish that will impress your family and friends. You can use 2 tablespoons of dried basil if you can't get fresh basil, or even 3 tablespoons of pesto. *Buon appetito*!

1 Make the pasta. Combine the flour with the dried basil and a large pinch of salt on your work surface and make a well in the centre. Beat the eggs in a bowl with the egg yolk, oil and fresh basil, then pour into the well. Gradually draw the flour into the well with a fork, then work with your hands to a soft, pliable dough. Divide into quarters, wrap in clingfilm and leave in a cool place for 30 minutes.

2 Roll each piece of dough through a pasta machine with the rollers on their widest setting. Fold each piece into thirds and pass through the machine again. Repeat twice or until the dough is smooth and shiny. Continue to pass the dough through the machine, gradually decreasing the space between the rollers until the desired thinness is achieved. Now cut the dough into long, thin ribbons and spread them out, without touching, on the work surface. Dust lightly with flour and leave to dry.

3 While the pasta is drying, place the salmon and milk in a frying pan, bring to the boil and simmer for 3 minutes. Turn off the heat and leave the salmon to continue cooking for about 5 minutes until the flesh is opaque. Remove it from the milk and flake into large chunks. Strain the milk and reserve.

4 Make the sauce. Melt the butter in a saucepan on medium heat, add the flour and mix to a paste. Cook for 1 minute, stirring, then pour in the warm milk a little at a time, whisking vigorously. Season to taste and continue cooking for a couple of minutes, stirring frequently, until glossy and smooth. Remove from the heat.

5 Bring a large saucepan of water to the boil on high heat. Tip in 1 tbsp salt, then drop in the pasta. Stir, then boil for 3 minutes. Meanwhile, add the cheese, parsley and garlic to the sauce and taste for seasoning. Now gently stir in the salmon and prawns and heat through.

6 Drain the pasta and divide between 4 warmed bowls. Spoon the sauce on top and garnish with sprigs of basil.

Andrew Lloyd

thai-style prawn toasts

20 uncooked prawns, peeled, deveined
   and roughly chopped
1 large bunch fresh coriander, roughly
   chopped (stalks 'n' all)
1 large clove garlic, roughly chopped
1 heaped tsp salt
1 heaped tsp ground white pepper
5–6 slices white bread from a large loaf
about 6 tbsp sesame seeds
vegetable oil, for deep-frying

This Thai version of prawn toast, called *kanom pung na goong*, is a real winner. It's so much nicer than the Chinese equivalent because you can actually see and taste the beautiful prawn mixture. You can make them well in advance and drop them in the hot oil at the last moment. They only take a couple of minutes to cook.

1 Put the prawns, coriander, garlic and seasonings into a food processor and blitz to a paste.

2 Cut the crusts off the bread, then cut each slice into 8 bite-sized pieces. Spread the paste over one side of each piece, then dip the paste side into the sesame seeds until evenly coated.

3 Heat the oil in a wok or deep-fat fryer to 180–190°C, or until a cube of bread turns golden in about 30 seconds. Lower the prawn toasts into the hot oil and deep-fry for 1–2 minutes on each side until golden brown. It is best to do this in batches so that the pan does not become overcrowded.

4 Lift the prawn toasts out of the oil with a slotted spoon, drain on kitchen paper and leave to stand for a few minutes before serving.

Dane Bowers

chargrilled langoustines with chilli & lime mayo

24 langoustines, peeled
olive oil
1 small red onion, finely sliced
1 red chilli, finely chopped (with or
    without seeds according to taste)
1 green chilli, finely chopped (with or
    without seeds according to taste)
juice of 1 lime
1 x 100g bag rocket salad

FOR THE MAYO
100g mayonnaise
finely grated zest and juice of 1 unwaxed lime
1 red chilli, finely chopped (with or without
    seeds according to taste)
1 green chilli, finely chopped (with or without
    seeds according to taste)

SERVES FOUR

I chose langoustines because ... well, they just sound posh! They're little prawn-type things that look like mini lobsters. The hardest part is taking off the heads and getting them clean but they are so tasty! For the chilli and lime mayonnaise, the hotter the better. Even if you don't like too much spice, the lime juice just calms it a little. All in all, this is a great dish to start any meal.

1 Put the mayonnaise into a bowl and mix in the lime zest and juice. Add the chillies and stir well. Cover and keep in the fridge until ready to serve.

2 Heat a griddle pan until hot. Toss the langoustines in 2 tbsp olive oil, lay them on the griddle pan and cook on medium heat for 1–2 minutes on each side. Remove from the pan and keep hot.

3 Now put the onion and chillies into the pan, with some olive oil if necessary, and toss until softened and lightly coloured – about 5 minutes. Transfer to a bowl and mix in the lime juice.

4 Divide the rocket between 4 plates and top with the langoustines, onion and chillies. Serve with the mayo on the side.

Jay Davies

mackerel california rolls & tuna sashimi

250g sushi rice
330ml cold water
2 tbsp rice vinegar
2 tbsp caster sugar
large pinch of salt
1 bamboo rolling mat
4 sheets sushi nori
3 tbsp mayonnaise
1 tbsp wasabi paste
1 x 200g fresh or marinated mackerel fillet,
   skinned and cut crossways into thin strips
   (available at Japanese foodshops)
7.5cm piece cucumber, peeled, deseeded
   and cut into thin strips
1 x 200g very fresh sashimi-grade tuna
   steak (available at Japanese foodshops),
   well chilled

TO SERVE
Japanese soy sauce
pickled ginger
wasabi paste

SERVES FOUR

Mackerel rolls and tuna sashimi are perfect together. It takes many years to become a sushi chef and I'm still trying, but it's a fun dish to make. The saying 'good things come in small packages' could not be truer for this healthy starter.

1 Put the rice into a medium saucepan, pour in the cold water and leave to soak for 30 minutes.

2 Bring the pan of rice to the boil on medium heat, cover with the pan lid and simmer on low heat for 10 minutes without stirring. Remove from the heat and leave for 15 minutes without lifting the lid.

3 Meanwhile, mix the vinegar, sugar and salt in a small bowl.

4 Turn the rice into a large bowl, add the vinegar solution and stir with a wooden spoon until the rice becomes sticky. Cover with a damp cloth and allow to cool.

5 To make the rolls, place the rolling mat on the work surface with the bamboo running horizontally in front of you. Place a sheet of nori shiny-side down on the mat, positioning it close to the edge nearest to you. Spread one-quarter of the rice over the nori, pressing it down until it is about 5mm thick. Leave a 2cm gap at the edge furthest away from you.

6 Mix the mayonnaise with the wasabi paste and spread one-quarter of this mix in a line across the middle of the rice. Put one-quarter of the mackerel and cucumber strips on top of the mayonnaise.

7 Lift up the end of the mat nearest to you and roll the nori around the rice and filling, rolling away from you and pressing the mat around the roll to keep as tight a shape as possible. Seal the edges of the nori with water. Repeat with the remaining ingredients to make 4 rolls altogether, then leave to stand for 30 minutes.

8 With a wet, very sharp knife, trim off the ends of the rolls to neaten them. Cut each roll in half, then cut each half into 3 or 4 equal pieces to get 6 or 8 pieces from each roll.

9 Take the tuna from the fridge and cut into very thin slices against the grain. Arrange on a platter with the sushi rolls and serve immediately, with soy sauce, pickled ginger and wasabi paste.

Russell Dunmore

prawn soup americaine with tomato & basil pastries

2 tbsp olive oil
1 stick celery, trimmed and finely diced
1 carrot, finely diced
4 very ripe tomatoes, finely diced
300g uncooked prawns, peeled, deveined
   and roughly chopped
50ml vermouth
50ml brandy
600ml fish stock
75ml double cream

FOR THE PASTRIES
100g puff pastry
10 small cherry tomatoes, quartered
1 tbsp olive oil
5 large fresh basil leaves, cut into fine strips
1 clove garlic, crushed

SERVES SIX

My brother-in-law Roberto is a chef and he inspired me to come up with this recipe. It sounds posh but it is actually an easy dish to make. There are no secret techniques involved, except to squash and squeeze as much flavour out of the ingredients as possible. My top tips would be to use very ripe tomatoes and a very fine sieve. In the programme I used this recipe as an amuse-bouche but it's really versatile and you can also use it as a sauce to make a nice pasta dish like spaghetti with prawns or lobster – lovely!

1 Heat the oil in a large non-stick saucepan until hot. Add the celery, carrot, tomatoes, prawns and seasoning to taste. Cover and sweat on medium heat for 10 minutes or until the vegetables have softened, stirring occasionally.

2 Pour in the vermouth, brandy and stock. Bring to the boil and simmer until the liquid is reduced by around a third – this should take about 10 minutes. Remove from the heat and leave to cool a little.

3 Tip the contents of the pan into a blender and whiz to a purée. Now work the purée through a fine sieve into a clean saucepan, pressing really hard to force through as much of the vegetable and prawn juice as possible. Set aside until ready to serve.

4 Preheat the oven to 200°C/Gas 6. Cover a baking sheet with non-stick baking parchment.

5 Make the pastries. Roll out the pastry on a lightly floured surface to around the thickness of a £1 coin. Cut into 20 x 4cm squares. Put the squares on the baking sheet.

6 Toss the tomatoes in a bowl with the olive oil, basil, garlic, a pinch of salt and plenty of freshly ground black pepper. Divide the tomato mixture equally between the pastry squares. Bake for 12–15 minutes until the pastry is well risen and golden.

7 Meanwhile, add the cream to the soup and heat through, stirring. Taste for seasoning before ladling into 6 warmed bowls. Serve at once, with the pastries.

Ian Jones

smoked fish soufflés with watercress salad

250g smoked haddock fillet (I buy
   line-caught and undyed)
2 tbsp dry white wine
1 bay leaf
350ml whole milk
2 tbsp polenta
30g salted butter, plus extra for greasing
30g plain flour
1 tsp English mustard powder
50g mature Cheddar cheese, grated
4 medium eggs, separated

FOR THE SALAD
1 x 110g bag mixed watercress, spinach
   and rocket
extra virgin olive oil
balsamic vinegar

SERVES SIX

This recipe was inspired by *River Cottage*'s Hugh Fearnley-Whittingstall, my hero. When choosing your smoked fish, use the undyed kind. Also grease your ramekins well, which stops the soufflé from sticking to the sides of the dish. I used polenta to line the dishes, since it had a nice crunch to it.

1 Place the fish in a large shallow pan with the wine, bay leaf and milk. Cover and bring to a simmer on medium heat, then poach gently for 5 minutes. Remove the fish, strain the milk and reserve. Flake the fish, removing any skin and bones, and set aside.

2 Preheat the oven to 200°C/Gas 6. Generously butter 6 x 200ml soufflé dishes or ramekins and coat with the polenta. Stand the dishes in a roasting tin.

3 Melt the butter in a saucepan on medium heat, add the flour and stir to form a roux. Cook for 1 minute, stirring, then remove from heat and gradually add the fish milk, whisking vigorously after each addition. Return to the heat and bring to the boil, stirring, then simmer for about 2 minutes until thickened and smooth. Remove from the heat.

4 Add the mustard powder and cheese to the sauce and stir until melted and smooth, then beat in the egg yolks and gently fold in the fish. Season with black pepper to taste.

5 Using electric beaters, whisk the egg whites to stiff peaks in a large bowl. Now slowly and gently fold the egg whites into the fish and cheese mixture until evenly incorporated.

6 Spoon the mixture into the soufflé dishes, then run the tip of a sharp knife around the edge of each soufflé to release it from the side of the dish (this will help the soufflés rise). Pour cold water into the roasting tin to come halfway up the sides of the dishes. Bake for 20 minutes or until the soufflés are well risen and golden on top, with a slight wobble in the centre when shaken.

7 Meanwhile, toss the salad leaves in a bowl with a drizzle each of olive oil and balsamic vinegar and salt and pepper to taste. Serve the soufflés immediately, with the salad on the side.

William Henry

scallops with broad bean purée

400g shelled broad beans (fresh or frozen)
125ml double cream
1 clove garlic, roughly chopped
2 tbsp grated Parmesan cheese
2 tbsp chopped fresh mint
3 tbsp olive oil
1 tbsp lemon juice
15 large scallops
fresh mint sprigs, to garnish

I wanted to challenge my guests with this starter. Scallops are difficult to do well but the broad bean purée and lemon juice made the dish just right. Don't cook the scallops for too long as they will become tennis balls!

1 Plunge the broad beans into a saucepan of boiling salted water, bring back to the boil and simmer for 4 minutes or until tender. Drain and rinse under cold running water, then slip off the skins with your fingers.

2 Purée the broad beans in a blender with the cream, garlic, Parmesan and mint. Taste and add seasoning to your liking. Transfer to a pan and set aside.

3 Make a dressing by whisking together 2 tbsp of the olive oil with the lemon juice. Season well and set aside.

4 Toss the scallops in seasoning to taste. Heat the remaining 1 tbsp olive oil in a large frying pan until hot and cook the scallops for 1 minute. Meanwhile, quickly reheat the broad bean purée, stirring vigorously.

5 Turn the scallops over and cook for another minute.

6 Divide the broad bean purée between 5 plates and arrange 3 scallops on top of each serving. Drizzle with the dressing, garnish with mint sprigs and serve immediately.

Maggie Thompson

camembert, apricot & ginger tartlets

FOR THE PASTRY
175g plain flour
pinch of salt
85g lard, cut into small cubes
about 1½ tbsp cold water
butter, for greasing

FOR THE FILLING
2 tbsp olive oil
knob of butter
2.5cm piece fresh root ginger, finely chopped
1 red onion, finely chopped
50g ready-to-eat dried apricots, finely chopped
8 slices ripe Camembert cheese (about 125g total weight)

TO SERVE
25g rocket
2–3 tbsp balsamic dressing

SERVES FOUR

This is perfect as a starter or light supper. The mixture of sweet and savoury works really well together. It's quick to make but gives the impression that you have gone to loads of effort. You could replace the filling with a good-quality caramelized onion chutney, ginger and garlic paste, and use ready-made shortcrust pastry.

1 Make the pastry. Sift the flour and salt into a large bowl, drop in the cubes of lard and rub them into the flour until the mixture looks like breadcrumbs. Now add about 1½ tbsp cold water a little at a time, mixing it in with a fork to make a firm dough. Wrap the dough in clingfilm and chill in the fridge for about 15 minutes.

2 Preheat the oven to 190°C/Gas 5. Butter 4 x 9cm loose-bottomed tartlet tins.

3 Remove the clingfilm and roll the dough out on a lightly floured surface until about 2mm thick. Cut 4 x 11cm discs out of the pastry, then use to line the tartlet tins. Prick the pastry on the bottom with a fork and line the tarts with greaseproof paper or foil and fill with baking beans.

4 Bake blind for 15 minutes, then remove the paper and beans and bake for a further 5–8 minutes until the pastry is cooked.

5 Make the filling while the pastry is baking. Heat the oil and butter in a frying pan until the butter is foaming and sauté the ginger and onion on medium heat for 5–8 minutes until soft and golden. Add the apricots and stir-fry for 1 minute, then season to taste with salt and pepper.

6 Spoon the filling into the tartlet cases and top with the Camembert slices. Place in the oven and bake for 5–8 minutes until the cheese has melted.

7 To serve, toss the rocket with the dressing and divide between 4 plates. Remove the tartlets from the tins, place on top of the salad and serve straightaway.

Dave Spinx

crab cakes

1 tbsp butter
1 tbsp olive oil
1 small onion, finely chopped
1 red pepper, cored, deseeded and finely
    chopped
1 stick celery, finely chopped
1 tsp finely chopped garlic
1 tsp Italian seasoning or Mediterranean
    mixed herbs
1 tsp Cajun seasoning (Bart's is the brand I use)
80g fresh white breadcrumbs
2 tbsp mayonnaise, more if needed
1 tsp Creole or Dijon mustard
225g fresh white crabmeat
1 medium egg
125ml milk
dash of lemon juice (optional)
vegetable oil, for frying

SERVES FIVE TO SIX

Crab cakes have always been a classic dish, but when you add Cajun spices they become something special. Substitute eggs for the mayo to bind the mixture together and the crab cakes become extra-tasty too. If you fancy a mixture of prawns or other fish then go for it! These are great for parties because you can do all the preparation early and fry them up later. Enjoy!

1 Heat the butter and oil in a frying pan and sauté the onion, pepper and celery on low to medium heat for 5 minutes or until soft.

2 Add the garlic and seasonings, tip into a bowl and stir in half the breadcrumbs. Add the mayonnaise and mustard and mix well, then fold in the crabmeat until evenly blended. Add more mayonnaise if the mixture seems dry – it should be sticky enough to form patties.

3 Divide the mixture to form 5–6 patties (like burgers). Place on a plate and chill in the fridge for at least 30 minutes.

4 Whisk the egg and milk together in a shallow dish and add a dash of lemon juice, if you like. Spread the remaining breadcrumbs out on a plate. Dip each patty in the egg, then coat with the breadcrumbs.

5 Pour enough oil into a deep frying pan to cover the bottom of the pan. Place the pan on medium heat and heat until the oil is hot, then carefully place the patties in the pan and fry for 2–3 minutes on each side or until golden, turning once. Don't go too far from the stove – 2 minutes passes fast.

6 Remove the crab cakes with a fish slice and place on several layers of kitchen paper to remove the excess oil. Serve hot.

main courses

Veronica O'Connor

roast marmalade chicken

8–12 chicken thighs (on or off the bone),
    skin and excess fat removed
1 tbsp thick-cut Seville orange marmalade
1 tbsp Dijon mustard
2 red onions, quartered
1 small unwaxed orange, cut into wedges
1 tbsp olive oil

SERVES FOUR

The hardest part about making this recipe is opening the jar of marmalade! I prefer using chicken thighs as I think they give a better flavour, which contrasts nicely with the bitter sweetness of the Seville oranges. A sprinkle of fresh flat-leaf parsley before serving makes this dish look even prettier!

1 Preheat the oven to 200°C/Gas 6.

2 Season the chicken with salt and pepper. Mix the marmalade and mustard together in a small bowl to make a thick paste and brush all over the chicken.

3 Put the chicken in a roasting tin with the onions and orange wedges and drizzle with the oil. Place in the oven and roast for 50 minutes, basting 2–3 times.

4 Remove the tin from the oven and baste the chicken well with the juices, then pour the juices into a small saucepan. Return the chicken, onions and orange to the oven and roast for a further 10 minutes.

5 Meanwhile, bring the juices to the boil on medium to high heat, then simmer for about 5 minutes until reduced and thickened slightly, stirring frequently. Taste the sauce for seasoning and serve hot, with the chicken and onions.

Dave Spinx

chicken suprêmes stuffed with italian cheese & ham

4 chicken suprêmes (breasts with part
    of the wing bone attached), skin on
100g Taleggio cheese, rind removed and
    cut into 4 equal pieces
4 slices Parma ham (not horrible packet
    stuff, get it sliced at a good deli)
2 tbsp olive oil

FOR THE SAUCE
300ml good fresh chicken stock
100ml dry white wine
1 small clove garlic, crushed
2 tsp Dijon mustard

SERVES FOUR

This recipe was inspired by my local Italian restaurant. You will need some good chicken suprêmes – get your butcher to prepare them for you. When cooking, pan fry the chicken till the skin is golden brown and crispy before putting in the oven. Make sure that the cuts are facing upwards, so that the cheese won't leak out. Yum!

1 Preheat the oven to 200°C/Gas 6.

2 Make a deep pocket in each chicken breast, starting by cutting along the length of the thinnest side of the meat.

3 Roll each piece of cheese in a slice of ham and stuff inside the chicken.

4 Heat the oil in a frying pan until hot and sear the chicken skin-side down on medium to high heat until golden brown, about 5 minutes. Transfer to a roasting tray and roast for 20–25 minutes or until the chicken is cooked through.

5 Meanwhile, make the sauce. Put the stock, wine and garlic into a saucepan and bring to the boil on high heat. Continue boiling until the liquid has reduced by half, about 10 minutes, then strain into a clean pan. Whisk in the mustard on low heat and add seasoning to taste.

6 Let the chicken rest out of the oven for 5 minutes before serving with the sauce poured over and around it.

Alastair James

moroccan lamb

12 lamb cutlets, trimmed of excess fat
olive oil
splash of red wine
300ml beef stock

FOR THE MARINADE
8 tbsp olive oil
2 tsp ground cumin
1 tsp ground cinnamon
½ tsp freshly grated nutmeg
good pinch or two of dried red chilli flakes,
    to taste
2 tbsp finely chopped fresh coriander
large knob of fresh root ginger, grated
    or crushed
squeeze of runny honey

SERVES FOUR

Make sure the lamb is marinated for at least 6 hours so it absorbs all the flavour of the spices. If you get the spice quantities right for the lamb it'll taste as if you're in another country. The smell from the kitchen alone will be enough to make your guests feel like they're dining out in a Kasbah – they'll be going home on camels.

1 Mix all the marinade ingredients together in a bowl. Place the lamb cutlets in a shallow dish and brush with the marinade until coated all over. Cover and leave to marinate in the fridge for at least 6 hours, overnight if possible.

2 When you are ready to cook, take the cutlets out of the fridge and let them come to room temperature for about an hour.

3 Heat a little oil in a large frying pan until hot and fry the lamb cutlets on medium heat for 2–3 minutes on each side. It's best to do this in 2–3 batches or the pan will be overcrowded. After frying, rest the meat in a warm place while you make the jus.

4 Deglaze the pan with a splash of red wine, scraping hard to release the sticky bits from the bottom. Pour in the stock and increase the heat to high. Bubble rapidly, stirring constantly, until reduced and thickened slightly, then season to taste.

5 Place 3 lamb cutlets on each of 4 warmed plates, spoon the jus over and serve straightaway.

David Bell

roast fillet of beef with king prawns, red wine gravy & rösti

1kg fillet of beef, tied with string
25g butter
12 uncooked king prawns, peeled and deveined
1 clove garlic, crushed

FOR THE GRAVY
250ml good red wine
400ml fresh beef stock
20g cold unsalted butter, cut into small cubes
Worcestershire sauce, to taste

FOR THE RÖSTI
500g potatoes, such as Maris Piper or Desirée
1 bunch spring onions, trimmed and finely chopped
handful of fresh flat-leaf parsley, leaves finely chopped
1 medium egg, beaten
1 tbsp olive oil
25g butter

SERVES FOUR

At first glance the mix of ingredients can seem unusual, but they complement each other extremely well. Both steak and seafood fans can appreciate this dish! Good meat and prawns are essential, so don't scrimp and buy the best ingredients you can. It may be worth speaking to your butcher and fishmonger beforehand to ensure you get the freshest produce. Getting everything synchronized can be a pain so timing is everything with this recipe.

1 For the gravy, pour the wine into a medium saucepan and bring to the boil on high heat. Continue boiling until reduced by about one-third, then pour in the stock and boil rapidly until the mixture has reduced by about half – it should be slightly syrupy. Remove from the heat and set aside until later.

2 Preheat the oven to 200°C/Gas 6. Lightly oil a baking sheet.

3 For the rösti, peel the potatoes and grate them coarsely (you need about 350g grated potato). Wrap in a tea towel and squeeze out the excess water. Place the potatoes in a bowl with the spring onions, parsley and salt and pepper to taste. Mix well and add enough of the beaten egg to bind the ingredients together. Shape into 4 discs using a 9cm plain pastry cutter, about 2cm deep.

4 Heat the oil and butter in a non-stick frying pan until the butter is foaming. Place the rösti in the pan and fry on medium heat for about 4 minutes on each side until golden, turning once. Transfer to the baking sheet, place in the oven and roast for 30 minutes.

5 Meanwhile, season the beef, place in a roasting tin and roast for 25 minutes for rare meat, 30 minutes for medium-rare. When the meat is done to your liking, take it out of the tin and leave to rest in a warm place for 10 minutes.

6 Heat the butter in a frying pan until foaming and lightly fry the prawns with the garlic for 3–5 minutes, just until they turn pink. Reheat the gravy and whisk in the cold butter and a few drops of Worcestershire sauce to taste.

7 Slice the beef and arrange on 4 warmed plates. Top the meat with the prawns and drizzle with the gravy. Serve at once, with the rösti on the side.

Natalie Carter

marengo-style chicken

3 tbsp olive oil
4 skinless, boneless chicken breasts
2 onions, finely sliced
4 cloves garlic, finely chopped
1 mild red chilli, deseeded and finely chopped
1 tsp paprika
200ml dry white wine
1 x 400g can chopped tomatoes
1½ tsp each dried oregano, basil, rosemary
   and thyme
8 uncooked crayfish tails, peeled
8 uncooked king prawns, peeled
4 ripe vine tomatoes, quartered

SERVES FOUR

This is a regal dish inspired by Napoleon after the Battle of Waterloo. If the legend is to be believed, Napoleon's personal chef was ordered to cook up a feast fit for a king, or more aptly an army, and threw together a mixture of tomato, egg and chicken into a dish of soaked bread. The idea inspired me but I wasn't keen on the bread or eggs, and also wanted to add more flavour to give a slight Mediterranean–Caribbean twist. My fiancé was born in Jamaica so a Caribbean twist features heavily in our cooking!

1 Heat 2 tbsp of the olive oil in a large flameproof casserole or saucepan until hot. Season the chicken and brown on medium heat, about 5 minutes. Remove from the pan with a slotted spoon and set aside.

2 Heat the remaining 1 tbsp in the pan and sweat the onions, garlic and chilli on low heat until the onions begin to soften, 5–8 minutes. Add the paprika and stir for a minute or two, then pour in the wine and bring to the boil, stirring. Now simmer, stirring occasionally, until the liquid has reduced and is just covering the onions. Add the canned tomatoes and half a can of water, stir in the herbs and cover the pan. Simmer on low heat for 10 minutes, stirring occasionally.

3 Add the browned chicken to the pan and turn the pieces so that they become coated in the sauce. Cover and simmer gently for 20 minutes, turning the pieces over halfway.

4 Add the crayfish, prawns and fresh tomatoes, making sure that they are submerged in the sauce. Cover the pan again and simmer for another 10 minutes. Taste the sauce for seasoning at the end.

5 Serve the chicken hot, with the shellfish and sauce spooned over and around it.

Stuart Hudson

monkfish with wild garlic & capers

75g caster sugar
100ml white wine vinegar
2 tbsp drained capers
1 small bunch wild garlic
handful of walnuts
splash of extra virgin olive oil
rock salt
25g butter
4 pieces monkfish fillet (about 200g each)
cayenne pepper
watercress and rocket, to serve

This is a recipe inspired by local ingredients: wild garlic grows everywhere in Yorkshire and I love it. The 'pesto' has an intense flavour and, if you have any left over, works well spread on crusty bread.

1 Put the sugar, vinegar and capers into a small saucepan and heat gently, stirring, until the sugar has dissolved. Increase the heat and boil until the liquid is reduced and syrupy, about 5 minutes. Take care not to boil too long or the syrup will turn to caramel.

2 Using a mortar and pestle, pound the wild garlic and walnuts together to make a kind of rough pesto, using a splash of olive oil to loosen the mixture. I also like to use a little rock salt, both as a seasoning and as an abrasive element to help the mix.

3 Preheat the oven to 180°C/Gas 4.

4 Melt the butter in an ovenproof, non-stick frying pan and quickly fry the monkfish fillets on medium to high heat until just coloured on each side – about 5 minutes in total. Season with a tiny pinch of cayenne pepper, then transfer the pan of fish to the oven and roast for 8–10 minutes. Don't cook for longer than this or the fish will be dry.

5 In the meantime, mix the caper syrup and pesto together in a saucepan and place the pan on low heat to warm the mix through.

6 Remove the fish from the oven and drain the cooking liquid into the wild garlic and caper mixture, to loosen it.

7 To serve, place a spoonful of the wild garlic and caper mixture in the centre of 4 warmed plates. Place the monkfish on top, or slice the fish and fan the pieces out. Serve straightaway, with a little watercress and rocket on the side.

Lee Stafford

pancetta-wrapped chicken with sausage stuffing & asparagus

4 large skinless, boneless chicken breasts
4 Lincolnshire sausages
50g young spinach leaves, finely chopped
25g rocket leaves, finely chopped
1 shallot, finely chopped
4 baby plum tomatoes, finely chopped
½ tsp dried red chilli flakes
8 asparagus tips
12 slices pancetta

This is a dish that is packed with taste and looks good on the plate, especially when it's sliced down the middle to reveal the stuffing and asparagus. It's always a big favourite with my friends.

1 Preheat the oven to 200°C/Gas 6.

2 Butterfly each chicken breast: make a slit along the length of the thinnest side of the meat with a sharp knife, then cut through the flesh to the other side and open the breast out flat.

3 Remove the skins from the sausages and place the sausagemeat in a bowl with the spinach, rocket, shallot, tomatoes and chilli flakes. Season to taste and mix well.

4 Bring a pan of salted water to the boil and cook the asparagus tips for 2 minutes, then drain and dry well.

5 Lay 3 overlapping slices of pancetta on a board and place 1 chicken breast in the centre with its cut-side uppermost. Spread one-quarter of the sausage mixture over the chicken breast and place 2 asparagus tips on top. Fold the chicken over to enclose the stuffing, wrapping the pancetta tightly and evenly around. Repeat to make 4 parcels altogether.

6 Place the chicken parcels on a baking tray and roast for 30 minutes. Leave to stand in a warm place for 5 minutes before serving.

desserts

Ali McKernan

lemon posset

600ml double cream
150g caster sugar or vanilla sugar
juice of 2 large lemons

Talk about a doddle! This cheeky little lemon posset delivers a crafty citrus smack and it's also possibly the simplest dessert you may ever make. Yes ... yes ... YES!

1 Pour the cream into a large saucepan and add the sugar. Warm gently on low heat, stirring until the sugar has dissolved.

2 Increase the heat and bring the cream to the boil, then boil for exactly 3 minutes, without stirring.

3 Remove the pan from the heat and whisk in the lemon juice. Strain into a jug, and pour into 6 ramekins or small glasses. Cool, then refrigerate for 2–3 hours until set before serving.

Stuart Hudson

pistachio cake with rhubarb sorbet

150g pistachio nuts
65g polenta
35g plain flour
1 tsp baking powder
150ml olive oil
50g butter, melted, plus extra for greasing
3 medium eggs
200g caster sugar
finely grated zest and juice of
    1 unwaxed orange

FOR THE SORBET
500g rhubarb, trimmed and chopped
4 tbsp water
1 tsp liquid glucose
100g caster sugar

This recipe came from a drunken, post-barbeque conversation about carrot cake! It was dictated to me at the time, so whoever gave me the recipe – thank you very much! Be sure to track down Yorkshire rhubarb: it's the best.

1 For the sorbet, put the rhubarb into a saucepan with the water, liquid glucose and sugar. Bring slowly to the boil, stirring until the sugar has dissolved, then poach gently for about 5 minutes or until the rhubarb is tender. Allow to cool slightly, then purée in a blender. Churn the mixture in an ice-cream maker, then place in an airtight container in the freezer until required (it will keep for up to a month).

2 Preheat the oven to 180°C/Gas 4. Grease a 20cm springform or loose-bottomed cake tin and line the bottom with greaseproof paper.

3 Make the cake. Coarsely grind the pistachios in a small food processor, using the pulse button so that they are not too finely ground – they still want a bit of texture. Tip into a bowl and mix in the polenta, flour and baking powder.

4 Mix the olive oil and butter together in a bowl. In a separate large bowl and using electric beaters, whisk the eggs and sugar together until the mixture is thick enough to hold a ribbon trail when the beaters are lifted. Slowly stir in the oil and butter mixture, then gently fold in the polenta mixture along with the orange zest and juice until evenly incorporated.

5 Pour the mixture into the prepared tin and bake for 55–60 minutes, or until the top is golden and a skewer inserted in the centre comes out clean. Remove from the oven and leave to cool for 10 minutes in the tin before removing and placing on a wire rack to cool completely.

6 To serve, cut the cake into 8 slices and place a slice on each of 8 plates with a scoop of sorbet. Serve straightaway.

Dave Spinx

lemon polenta cake with limoncello syrup

250g butter, softened
250g caster sugar
3 medium eggs, at room temperature
100g fine polenta (cornmeal)
250g ground almonds
1 tsp baking powder
finely grated zest of 3 unwaxed lemons
juice of 1 lemon

FOR THE SYRUP
4 tbsp limoncello liqueur
3 tbsp icing sugar, sifted

SERVES SIX TO EIGHT

Most people come across polenta as a savoury ingredient but it can make a fabulous cake. I've made this dessert loads of times and everyone loves it! I usually serve it with a limoncello syrup but if you fancy Amaretto or ice cream … well, who am I to argue with that? Happy eating.

1 Preheat the oven to 160°C/Gas 3. Butter and base-line a 23cm springform or loose-bottomed cake tin.

2 Using electric beaters, cream the butter and sugar together until light and fluffy. Add the eggs one by one, beating well after each addition.

3 Fold in the polenta, almonds and baking powder followed by the lemon zest and juice. Spoon into the prepared tin and level the surface.

4 Bake for 60–70 minutes until the cake is risen and golden, covering the top with foil after 40 minutes if it starts to brown too much. To test if the cake is done, pierce the centre with a skewer – it should come out clean.

5 Remove the cake from the oven and leave to settle for about 10 minutes before removing from the tin.

6 Make the syrup by warming the liqueur and icing sugar in a pan on low heat, stirring constantly. Serve the cake warm, with a drizzle of limoncello syrup.

Harry Ioannou

orange crème caramel

1 large unwaxed orange
125g caster sugar
3 large eggs
120ml whole milk
220ml single cream
1 tsp vanilla extract
crème fraîche, to serve

I know crème caramel is supposed to be French but the Greeks adopted it as their own back in the 1940s when they first started arriving *en masse* in the UK. I doubt you will visit any Greek restaurant and not see it on the menu alongside *risogalo* (rice pudding) and *yaorti me meli* (yogurt with honey). The orange flavour was my idea to zest it up a bit. My mum thought I was mad messing around with it, but thought it was lovely when she tried it – mamma is never wrong!

1 Cut 5 thin slices from the orange, place in a pan and cover with water. Bring to the boil, then lower the heat and simmer for 20 minutes or until soft. Drain and reserve both the orange slices and the orange water.

2 Preheat the oven to 150°C/Gas 2. Stand a 21–22cm round baking dish or tin (about 4cm deep) in a roasting tin.

3 Tip the sugar into a medium saucepan and place on medium heat. Cook for 10–15 minutes until the sugar dissolves and turns a deep golden colour, shaking the pan occasionally. Slowly add 3 tbsp of the orange water, taking great care as the caramel will splash when the liquid hits the hot sugar. Swirl the pan around to mix everything together and put it back on low heat to get it to dissolve again if necessary.

4 Pour three-quarters of the caramel into the baking dish and swirl the dish around so that the caramel evenly covers the bottom. Pat the orange slices dry with kitchen paper, then place them on top of the caramel.

5 Beat the eggs in a large bowl and set aside. Stir the milk, cream and vanilla together in a jug.

6 Melt the remaining caramel in the pan on low to medium heat until runny again, then pour in about half the cream mixture, stirring all the time and making sure that the sugar remains liquid. It will go into lumps as the cold cream mixture is added, but will become smooth as the

caramel dissolves into the liquid. Stir constantly and do not allow to boil. When dissolved, stir in the rest of the cream mix, then remove from the heat.

7 Stir the contents of the pan into the eggs until smooth and evenly mixed. Strain this custard through a fine sieve into the dish over the oranges and caramel, then pour hot water into the roasting tin to come about halfway up the dish.

8 Place in the oven and bake for 30–35 minutes or until just starting to set – the centre should wobble slightly when the dish is shaken.

9 Carefully remove the dish from the roasting tin and allow to cool, then place in the fridge to set overnight.

10 To serve, run a thin knife around the inside edge of the dish and turn the crème caramel out upside-down on to a serving dish (you need a dish rather than a plate to catch the caramel). You will find that it comes out very easily and has a nice layer of caramel on top. Serve with crème fraîche.

Jan Leeming

soufflé milanaise au citron

3 medium eggs, separated
175g caster sugar
finely grated zest and juice of 2½ unwaxed
    lemons (100ml juice)
1 x 12g sachet gelatine powder
4 tbsp cold water
275–300ml double or whipping cream
toasted almond flakes, to decorate

I like a dessert with a tang to it. Although this one does have cream as an ingredient, I think the overall lemony taste cleanses the palate after a meal – especially as I serve food the French way and serve cheese after the main course and then the dessert. I can't remember how I came up with the recipe but I know I've been making it for over 40 years, as I demonstrated it on camera for a food programme in the 1970s.

1 Put the egg yolks and sugar into a non-stick saucepan with the lemon zest and juice. Whisk on very low heat until thickened, about 10 minutes, then pour into a large bowl and leave to cool.

2 Meanwhile, sprinkle the gelatine over the water in a small heatproof bowl. Leave until spongy, then stand the bowl in a pan of hot water and heat gently until the gelatine has dissolved, stirring occasionally.

3 Pour the cream into a bowl and whip to soft peaks. In a separate bowl, whisk the egg whites until stiff.

4 Stir the gelatine into the lemon mixture, then fold in the cream followed by the egg whites. When all the ingredients are evenly blended, spoon into a large serving bowl or 6 individual glasses and leave to set. Serve chilled, sprinkled with toasted almond flakes.

summer

Even if the weather disappoints in the summer, it's rare that the produce does. There's nothing better than eating your way through the full gamut of classic British fruit — from strawberries in June to raspberries in July and plums, sometimes even the first crunchy apples, at the tail end of August. There's also a feast of beans — French, runner, broad, green — plus plenty of other tasty vegetables.

When it comes to entertaining, it's all about barbeques and picnics (if the weather holds!). Summer's the perfect time for outdoor entertaining when it comes to birthdays or anniversaries, and make sure that Father's Day is also in your diary in June.

Vegetables

Asparagus (June)
Aubergine (August)
Beetroot
Broad beans (June/July)
Calabrese broccoli
Carrots
Cauliflower (July/August)
Celery (July/August)
Courgettes (July/August)
Cucumber
French beans (late July/August)
Lettuce
New potatoes
Peas (July/August)
Peppers (August)
Radishes (July)
Runner beans (late July/August)
Spinach
Sweetcorn (August)
Watercress

Fruit

Apples (August)
Apricots (August)
Black, red and white currants (July/August)
Blueberries (July/August)
Cherries
Gooseberries (June/July)
Loganberries (August)
Plums (August)
Raspberries (July/August)
Strawberries (June/July)

Meat

Grouse (August)

Fish

Crab
Dover sole (August)
Hake
Herring (August)
Lobster
Mullet (July/August)
Pilchards (August)
Plaice (July/August)
Prawns
Sardines (June)
Squid (July)

barbeques

The summer barbeque … In your mind's eye you can picture the scene: a group of friends lounging around in your garden; the buzz of laughter and chatter; the sun shining; the barbeque sizzling in the background; a non-stop supply of cold drinks.

Then you wake from your daydream and remember that this is Britain and there is a perpetual threat of rain right up to the moment you start cooking. But don't be put off – with the right amount of courage and forward-planning you can deal with anything that's thrown at you.

Let's go through what can go wrong – and how you can cope.

The weather: There are two types of barbie: impromptu and organized. The impromptu barbeque is perfect in every way, because in all likelihood the sun will be shining. Perfect in every way but one, that is. You and your other half/ flatmate will probably be the only ones there because it's the summer, it's last minute and all your mates are busy. Weddings, stag dos, hen dos, festivals (if you're young and trendy), opera (if you're not young and trendy) …

So, potentially the more enjoyable barbeque is the organized one: you can invite plenty of guests, make sure you get all the food in on time and buy beer on special offer. All in all, you can control everything — except for the capricious British climate, with which you get to play Russian roulette. No matter how much you fuss over the forecast and tap your barometer (all right, you haven't got a barometer, but you know what I mean), you can't do anything about the weather.

The food: If you can't control the weather, at least you can control the food to cope with all possibilities. Plan your menu with rain in mind so that your food can work just as easily under a grill, on the hob or in the oven — there's always the kitchen as back-up for when the storm clouds gather.

If you're lucky enough to have a barbeque with a lid, you could always still cook the food outside but entertain your guests inside. That's exactly what Richenda Hines did on *Come Dine With Me* to cook her spatchcock barbeque chicken. She regularly dashed in and out to check on the meat whilst also ensuring she was a good hostess. The chicken hit the spot with her diners, and she came second overall.

If the weather is looking good, you can be as simple or as exotic with the menu as you like — people are coming to celebrate the summer sun with you and won't have high expectations of the food. However, it's always nice to impress your friends with some marinated meat and fish, to give the day a feeling of fine-dining.

Side dishes: Think about these, since the food's going to hang around outside for a while so will be in danger of drying out, even if it's under cover. Bread is great in theory, but half an hour outside on a warm day and all it's good for is feeding the birds. Instead think couscous and roasted vegetables. If you're doing a salad, think about preparing a small one and topping it up throughout the day, adding the dressing at the last minute (unless you're a fan of curling lettuce, drowning in slowly fermenting dressing!).

The vegetarians: Don't fob them off with frozen veggie burgers. There's loads of interesting food that you can cook for them — haloumi kebabs, nut burgers, jacket potatoes, corn on the cob … the list goes on. Bear in mind the tongs and the grill — they're all going to be contaminated by meat juices, so keep a space on the barbeque for the veggie-friendly food, and have tools to match. The most dedicated veggies may insist on having their own barbeque so it's always worth buying a cheap disposable one just in case.

Pudding: Think about something simple that you can make early in the day and take straight out of the fridge when you're ready. Preferably something you can freeze if there are leftovers, which is possible after all those sausages and burgers.

Stay alert: It's all too easy to forget about the job in hand while you chat and end up with burnt food on your hands, as *Come Dine With Me* contestant Jay Davies almost discovered to his cost when he was playing host in Stoke. With his guests to keep sweet, he took his eye off the fish he was cooking on an open fire. Luckily he caught everything just in time, and the dessert grilled on the same open fire (see page 89) went down so well that he was eventually crowned joint winner.

The barbeque: It's an obvious piece of kit, really. But there are lots to choose from and, most importantly, two very different types of fuel: charcoal versus gas. Where you stand on this debate probably depends on how old you are.

The young, inexperienced barbequers among us will generally insist on charcoal, because it can't be a barbeque if you don't have that authentic charcoal flavour. Plus there's nothing more satisfying than starting up a fire — it's not a barbie if you're pressing an ignition button.

Your older, wiser barbeque chef will probably prefer gas. It heats up straight away, and there's none of this mucking around with coals for 40 minutes before you can even start cooking a sausage. The heat's easy to control, and who wants to deal with the nonsense of pausing the cooking every so often because you have to heat up more coals? You can even stir-fry on the gas ring, taking barbequing to a whole other level, and that barbeque taste is an old myth … lighter fuel taste, don't you mean? And let's not forget the real reason: you're a grown-up, you have a shed and you like the prestige of wheeling out that top-of-the-range, shiny barbeque which is only a bit smaller than the car.

The truth is, there are pros and cons for both. If you're the easily distracted type who likes chatting to your mates so much that by the time you turn your attention to the cooking the coals are generally colder than the beer, then gas is probably for you. (If you can afford it!)

Other useful bits of kit

A side-table: You'll be balancing plates, raw meat, different dishes and the rest of it, so it's useful to have something to put it all on. A side-table would be ideal, but if not then a chair works well, or a couple of boxes of beer.

The right tools: A friend once gave me a shiny, silver case, and inside was an amazing array of barbeque weapons: a brush to brush the meat with; another brush to brush the barbeque down with after you'd used it; big tongs; small tongs; a big knife; a flipper. It's brilliant, but probably a bit excessive. What you really need is a good flipper, a pair of tongs and a couple of small mesh baskets that you can stick a bit of salmon or tuna in, then place over the barbeque to prevent them sticking. If the worst comes to the worst and you can't lay your hands on any of this, then a knife and fork plus some heat-resistant gloves will do the trick.

A big bucket: Full of ice for you to chill beer in, as that way you don't have to keep going backwards and forwards to the fridge.

Plates: It's got to be either china or the outdoor, plastic variety if you're serving stuff that requires a bit of cutting up (we're talking pieces of meat, fillets of fish, not cheap burgers stuffed in buns). Floppy paper plates just won't work.

Cutlery: Beg, borrow or steal it (well, maybe not steal, but certainly beg or borrow), but always use metal knives and forks. Plastic is naff.

Glasses: Your guests will put their glasses down on the patio without thinking, and then they'll smash. So this is the one area – the only area – where you can get away with good-quality plastic.

Beer coolers: Perhaps tempting fate, these are only for use if you're lucky enough to have a hot day. The hotter the day, the colder the beer needs to be.

Other barbeque pointers

Here are a few quick pointers to cope with barbequing.

Dealing with wasps: They love sweet things. Take tomato ketchup, for example: serving it in a bowl for people to spoon on to their plates is great in theory, but it's a magnet for the little buzzing monsters, so keep it in the bottle.

There is a theory which says that bags of water hanging up (with or without coins inside them) will ward off annoying flies and wasps. Apparently it's something to do with light shining in their eyes and freaking them out, or their reflection being massive and scaring them away (and fair enough, who wouldn't be scared by a giant reflection of a wasp?). To date there has been no scientific research to prove or disprove any of this, so try it if you're desperate, but don't expect miracles. There are candles and repellent sprays on the market which claim to do the trick, and these are definitely worth having up your sleeve as a last-ditch attempt to ward off the little critters.

Who barbeques: The laziest man in the kitchen is miraculously transformed into Gordon Ramsay when the barbeque is fired up, fiddling, turning and prodding away. If your man needs to exert his masculinity by picking up the tools, don't fight it but relish the chance to catch up with your friends over a bottle of wine.

Guest etiquette: Don't let your guests barbeque. You wouldn't expect them to cook their main course if they came round for a dinner party, so the same goes here. And guests, you should never offer, not least because you may get stuck there for the rest of the afternoon.

Drink: Guests should bring a bottle. Cross your fingers that they bring more than they usually would for a dinner party, as they'll probably be staying longer and drinking more . . .

BBQ food has that smoky taste, so opt for red wines which aren't too complex but at the same time have enough body to cope with spicy food – Pinot Noir, Shiraz or Cabernet Sauvignon. As a rule, try to go for wines from hotter countries – America, Australia, Chile – since they're made using riper berries so will cope better with the big flavours.

If the sun's beaming down then a lot of people will be searching for the perfect white wine or well-chilled rosé. Go for something which has a bit of body to it, so it can compete with the red meats – Chablis and Chardonnay are good ones to try. When it comes to rosé, some love the sweet ones which taste like alcoholic Ribena while others love the drier ones, so we'll leave that to your personal choice.

The first barbeque of the year: Don't leave anything to chance when it comes to the equipment. The barbeque hasn't been used for months; it's been sitting in a damp shed; the ignition might not work any more; it could be covered in mould and will need a good clean. Dig it out well in advance of the big day and give it a test run.

Planning for the last barbeque: Whatever you do, clean the barbeque after every time you use it during August (when every barbeque could be your last one of the year). Otherwise, when you pull it out on that first baking hot weekend the following year, you'll open the lid to discover a layer of mould and bacteria that would make a biology laboratory proud. You can of course clean it then, but no matter how well you do the job, you'll always be left wondering what nasty little extras will be on the first batch of bangers that you serve up.

picnics

There is nothing more enjoyable than a delicious picnic on a gorgeous British summer's day. Here are a few ways to make it extra-special.

Where: Think scenic (but convenient, if there's a big group of you). If there are a lot of you then hopefully someone will volunteer to go ahead to bag the best spot. If no one does then offer the bribe that whoever does needn't worry about the food. Encourage them to colonize a bench (or benches) – picnic rugs are great, but after a while they are hard work on the old derrière (even if that derrière is well-padded), so it comes as welcome relief to have the alternative option of a bench to park a numb bum on.

Make sure you identify your meeting spot clearly: You're going to need some precise directions. Saying 'Meet at the big tree on the left of the path outside the tropical glasshouse at Kew Gardens' isn't very helpful when there are six different paths leading from the tropical glasshouse and each one has about a hundred big trees alongside it.

Ah, but everyone has a mobile phone, I hear you cry. That might be the case but don't forget that you're choosing a picturesque spot which might be miles from any mobile phone mast, so reception may not be guaranteed.

How to transport the drink: You're probably going to want to treat yourself to a cool drink or two, since nothing is more enjoyable than supping a chilled beer or glass of wine as you enjoy an alfresco dining experience. But it comes with a cost – to your back. The lure of the booze means you won't be driving, so by the time you're halfway to your destination you'll be cursing all those bottles which are the heaviest (and bulkiest) part of your picnic.

To save your back, do a bit of forward-planning. Find out which shops are nearest to your picnic location, then check out what booze they have in stock. If possible, pre-order what you want and ask them to chill it in advance. However if, on the day of your picnic, you ring through to someone who sounds like a bored A-Level student struggling to locate your reserved bottles, ditch the advance ordering and buy your supplies along the way.

Then there's the matter of what to drink: Bubbles are best, and white wine is a winner – but if you don't want to be obvious then try a rosé. Red is also an option if you've got lots of meaty food, but if the weather's warm it probably won't be everyone's first choice. Don't forget of course that the weather can change, so a flask full of tea or coffee is a handy standby.

Last but certainly not least, check you can drink where you're going. It may sound like an odd one, but drinking is now banned in more and more public spaces, particularly in cities. If you have any doubts, check in advance with the local council or park authorities.

Remember to take water. After all, you'll need a drop of the old H_2O if you're imbibing under a hot sun. Check out whether your picnic location has a drinking water supply. If it does, take lots of empty bottles to fill up; if it doesn't then use the nearest shops instead.

What to eat: Think hard about what to eat, since it has to travel well. Here are a few tips.

Salads: Leaves are good, but don't include chopped tomatoes otherwise you risk a soggy mess – whole cherry tomatoes are best. Similarly, carry the salad dressing separately then put it on at the last minute. If you don't, on a hot day your salad is soon going to look like it's been marinated. Picnics are perfect for more substantial salads, such as pasta, rice or couscous with vegetables – stuff that will sit happily in the bottom of a Tupperware container and not suffer from being jolted around.

Pastry: Great for holding tasty fillings together in the form of pies and quiches.

Nibbles: A must-have, because someone will always be late. If you tuck into the food before everyone arrives there will be none left for any latecomers, so keep everyone going with something to nibble on.

Firm desserts: Cheesecake sounds like a good idea, until it turns upside-down in your Tupperware and is smeared all over the lid. Brownies or cakes (with a dash of cream) – anything that holds firm and can be wrapped up as an extra precaution – are a good choice.

What to take and how to prepare

Picnic rugs (or chairs if you're driving or haven't got far to walk): If you're buying a rug from scratch, go for one with a plastic bottom to make it waterproof.

Glassware: Buy the sort that's bottom heavy, unless you want to be splashing out on even more wine to fill up those glasses which keep toppling over on the grass.

Plates: Use plastic or china ones, but no paper. They bend and everything falls off; they're also

bad for the environment. Don't forget dessert —
if you don't want to carry two sets of crockery
around, remember something to clean the plates
with between courses.

Knives, forks and spoons: The same applies here —
no plastic. Don't forget cutlery for dishing up.

Bottle opener, can opener and corkscrew:
The most important part of a picnic, bar none.
Food can always be eaten by hand, straight out
of the container. But wine, with a cork and no
corkscrew . . . imagine the frustration!

Of course you can get all of the above and
plenty more besides in one of those fancy
rucksacks that feature all the bits and bobs you
need for the perfect picnic. They do come at
a price though, and make sure there's room
to store the food alongside all those bottle
openers, plates, cutlery, etc.

Bottle stoppers: These are for wine and fizz, in
case you don't drink it all. Even if you think you're
bound to, they're still important to avoid spillages
if the bottles take a tumble. You don't want to be
2 miles from the nearest shop when your last
bottle is knocked over and the contents spilt.

The nitty gritty: Napkins, rubbish bags . . . obvious
really, but all too easy to forget.

Condiments: Salt, pepper, sauces: think about all
those things which you might need to spice up the
food.

Clothing: Remember the old saying, 'Four seasons
in one day.' Hopefully you won't see winter, but
there's always the risk of the weather turning a tad
autumnal, so pack a warmer layer. Don't forget the
sunscreen, hat and sunglasses for warmer days.

Packing: Put the heavy stuff in first, then the
delicate, lighter stuff in last, with a cool box/bag
option for the food which needs to be kept fresh.

The picnic as a date:
Picnics with friends are a great idea, but the picnic
can work just as well as a date.

First off, do your research: Ask your date's friends
what his/her favourite place is, then choose
accordingly (although make sure you check that
their favourite place isn't the one they used to
go to for years with their ex . . .).

Don't forget that the weather may intervene.
Even if the forecast predicts blazing sun, don't
believe it. Instead, choose a location which has a
handy indoor back-up option in the event of wet
weather. Equally, make sure that you can cope if the
weather is too hot to handle: a wide, treeless, open
space may sound ideal, but on a boiling day it can
seem like picnicking in the desert. Ensure there's
plenty of shade, and, if you're really thoughtful, bring
a spare hat for your date, even an umbrella if you
think finding shade is going to be tricky.

Cook and pack to impress: It's like dinner for
two, just outside. The food might be different,
but it's still an occasion to entertain someone
else, so if you've done the inviting, be sure to do
the preparation. If you're a man who's been invited
on the date then it's up to you to insist on carrying
all the heavy and awkward stuff — the booze, the
water, the picnic rug, plus the crockery and cutlery.
Do your research on what your date likes to drink,
but don't pack so much that it looks as if you're
trying to get him/her drunk!

This is also a chance to show off your culinary
talents, so if you're confident, try to turn it into a
three-course alfresco meal. Think of a light starter,
a pâté or terrine perhaps, or a cool meat salad
which you can put together on the spot. Pick a
simple main with a tasty side dish, and round it
off with his or her favourite cake for pudding.

Once you're packed and ready, meet your date
at a mutually agreeable location where you can be
transported to your surprise picnic spot. Then lay
out the rug, open the drink, tuck into the food and
enjoy yourself.

father's day

This usually falls on the third Sunday in June, and the tradition is apparently more than a hundred years old. To some people it is a complete commercial concoction, but enough people seem to enjoy it – last year we spent somewhere between £750 million and a billion pounds on our dads.

So what to do with dad? If he's the cook of the house then it's a chance to give him the day off – so see the notes on Mother's Day (pages 9 to 11), but reverse them. He will probably be the barbequer of the house, so you could turn the tables and cook one for him. Be careful not to make it too good and tasty though – nothing's more guaranteed to spoil a Father's Day than for him to realize that he's actually a bit rubbish at the art of barbequing.

If the weather's not good or he's not the cook of the house, the next best thing to do is rustle up something he always eats in restaurants, but rarely eats at home. Make a note of what he chooses when you go out for a meal, or ask him to tell you about the best meal he's eaten at a restaurant recently. He'll never suspect why, although if he's a typical bloke he'll be really vague and say, 'Some lamb thingy.' In this case you'll have to do a bit more research by contacting the restaurant he went to, but persevere and you might alight on something. Beware of one thing, though: replicating his favourite curry. The recipe will be a closely guarded secret and you'll never prise it out of them, so don't even think of trying to emulate it.

To round off the day, buy him his favourite beer, or maybe even buy a couple of new ones which are similar for him to try. Once the beer is chilled, turn on the telly and give him free reign over the remote control.

canapés, amuse-bouches & starters

Dan Redfern

melon with tomatoes & basil

15 baby cherry tomatoes
¼ ripe Galia melon
15 small fresh basil leaves
15 cocktail sticks

SERVES FIVE
This is a vegan- and vegetarian-friendly canapé. I use a slightly over-ripe melon for this. You have to eat them all in one go so you get all the flavours together.

1 Score a cross in the bottom of each tomato. Put the tomatoes into a large heatproof bowl and cover with boiling water. Leave for about 30 seconds, just until the skins start to peel back, then lift the tomatoes out into a sieve and hold under the cold tap until they are cool. Now peel off the skins with your fingers.

2 Remove and discard the melon seeds, then slide a sharp knife between the flesh and the skin to loosen the flesh. Cut the flesh across into slices and then into 15 small pieces.

3 Skewer a piece of melon on a cocktail stick. Now skewer a basil leaf and a cherry tomato on the same stick, one on top of the other. Repeat to fill 15 cocktail sticks altogether.

Stuart Hudson

pea velouté with coconut foam

50g butter
1 onion, chopped
2 sticks celery, chopped
½ leek, chopped
1 litre vegetable stock
750g shelled peas (fresh or frozen)
1 x 400ml can coconut milk, shaken well
before opening
1 tsp soya lecithin granules (available from
health food stores, they act as a stabilizer
for the foam)

I found this combination of pea and coconut online, so I used my own recipe for the velouté (a rich pea soup) and did a bit of research into foams. I was worried that the end result would be a little sweet, but it's really refreshing. In the summer you could also serve the pea velouté chilled.

1 Melt the butter in a large saucepan, add the onion and celery and cook for 4–5 minutes on medium heat until translucent but not brown. Add the leek and cook for a couple of minutes, then pour in 800ml of the stock.

2 Bring the stock to a rolling boil on high heat, add the peas and return to the boil, then simmer on medium heat for 3–4 minutes until tender. Add half the coconut milk and simmer for a further minute. Remove from the heat and leave to cool a little.

3 Tip the contents of the pan into a blender and whiz to a purée. Strain through a sieve into the rinsed-out pan, taste for seasoning and reheat gently.

4 While the soup is reheating, make the coconut foam. Mix the remaining stock and coconut milk in a small saucepan with the lecithin granules. Bring to the boil, then remove from the heat. Now use a stick blender to agitate the mixture until a foam appears on top – this will take several minutes, during which time you need to constantly work the stick gently up and down from the bottom of the pan to the top layer of liquid.

5 To serve, pour the velouté into 6 small glasses, cups or bowls (you don't want to fill them to the brim). Spoon some of the foam on top of each serving and serve immediately – the foam only holds up for about 5 minutes.

Kelly Hatt

chilled cucumber & dill soup

1 cucumber
1 spring onion, trimmed and coarsely chopped
350ml chicken stock
1 tbsp chopped fresh dill, or 1 tsp dried dill
125ml double cream
crushed ice, to serve

An amuse-bouche is an entrée to a meal, often served in high-quality restaurants with the chef's compliments. This is one of my favourites – it's easy and adds a touch of class to your dinner party. It must be served ice cold and presentation is the key. I serve this in shot glasses over crushed ice on a tray. Simple yet very effective.

1 Peel the cucumber and cut in half crossways. Now cut each piece into quarters lengthways and remove the seeds. Roughly chop the flesh.

2 Place the cucumber flesh and spring onion in a saucepan, pour in the stock and bring to the boil. Reduce the heat, cover and simmer gently for 10–15 minutes until the cucumber feels soft when pierced with a fork. Remove from the heat and leave to cool slightly, about 10 minutes.

3 Pour the contents of the pan into a blender or food processor, add the dill and cream and whiz to a smooth purée. Taste and add seasoning to your liking.

4 Decant the soup into a jug. Cover and chill in the fridge for at least 4 hours or until you are ready to serve – it will keep for up to 24 hours.

5 Whisk the chilled soup to make it smooth again, then pour into 6 chilled shot glasses (there may be enough for some second helpings depending on the size of your glasses). Spread crushed ice over a serving tray, push the shot glasses into the ice and serve at once.

Andrew Lloyd

spicy thai fish cakes

500g skinless white fish fillets, such as
  cod or haddock
2 tbsp Thai red curry paste
4 fresh Kaffir lime leaves, finely chopped,
  or finely grated zest of 2 unwaxed limes
1 tsp caster sugar
2 tsp cornflour
1 medium egg yolk
20 fine green beans, trimmed and very
  finely chopped
vegetable oil, for deep-frying

Wow, this has got to be one of my favourite Thai dishes. Called *tord mun* in Thai, all my friends absolutely love this! These little fish cakes are packed full of flavour. You can really taste every single ingredient. Make them small, almost one bite big. You can, if you wish, serve a dip of light soy sauce too. They don't need cooking for too long. You can make the fish cakes in advance, part-cook them and drop them back in the hot oil just before you want to serve them.

1 Check the fish for any stray bones and remove them, then cut the fish into chunks and place in a food processor with the curry paste, lime leaves or zest, sugar, cornflour and egg yolk. Blitz to a paste.

2 Turn the mixture on to a board and shape into 28–30 small balls, pressing the green beans into the centre. Flatten the balls slightly – they should be about 4cm across.

3 Heat the oil in a wok or deep-fat fryer to 180–190°C, or until a cube of bread turns golden in about 30 seconds. Lower the fish cakes into the hot oil and deep-fry for 2 minutes or until golden brown, turning once. It is best to do this in batches so that the pan does not become overcrowded.

4 Lift the fish cakes out of the oil with a slotted spoon, drain on kitchen paper and leave to stand for a few minutes before serving.

Gill Buley

chicken salad with tarragon & grapes

3–4 ready-roasted chicken breasts,
   total weight about 700g
2 tbsp mayonnaise
2 tbsp plain yoghurt
¼ tsp crushed garlic
1 tsp chopped fresh tarragon
1 x 500g bunch seedless green grapes
2 Little Gem lettuces, leaves separated
   and torn

TO SERVE
1 tbsp extra virgin olive oil
1 tbsp balsamic vinegar

SERVES FOUR

I love this recipe, and first discovered it back in the 1980s as it was a favourite of my mum's. Ideally it's best eaten when dining alfresco. There is nothing better than the taste of fresh green grapes with chicken, perfumed with the sweet fragrance of tarragon. It's the perfect recipe to bring the light taste, colour and fragrances of summer to your guests.

1 Shred the chicken meat into small pieces, discarding the skin and any bone.

2 Mix the mayonnaise in a large bowl with the yoghurt, garlic and tarragon. Slice the grapes in half and add half of them to the bowl with the chicken. Add the mayonnaise mixture to the chicken and grapes and mix well. Season with salt and pepper to taste, then divide the mixture into 4 equal portions.

3 Place a 10cm metal chefs' ring in the centre of a dinner plate (or use a plain 10cm pastry cutter, about 5cm deep). Put a layer of torn lettuce in the bottom of the ring, then add one of the chicken portions and press a layer of the reserved grapes on top, placing them skin-side up.

4 Carefully remove the ring while pressing gently on the grapes. Wipe the inside of the ring clean with kitchen paper, then make 3 more stacks in the same way.

5 To serve, whisk the oil and vinegar together and make a circular swirl of dressing around each stack. Serve straightaway, or keep in the fridge for up to 2 hours.

Amit Koshal

seekh kebabs

500g minced lamb
thumb-sized knob of fresh root ginger, grated
2 cloves garlic, crushed
1 tsp ground cumin
1 tsp garam masala
1 red chilli, finely chopped (with or without
    seeds according to taste)
handful of fresh coriander leaves, chopped
1 tsp mint sauce (from a jar)

FOR THE SAUCE
100ml crème fraîche
100ml soured cream
2 tbsp snipped fresh chives, or more to taste

What better way to whet your appetite than the smell and flavour of hot lamb kebabs? The spices and fresh coriander are pleasantly balanced with a hint of mint along with rich crème fraîche and chives. Be sure to make extra as they'll soon disappear. I think this is a great snack and a definite inclusion on the summer barbeque.

1 Make the sauce by mixing the crème fraîche in a bowl with the soured cream, then adding chives and salt and pepper to taste. Cover and keep in the fridge until serving time.

2 Preheat the grill on medium-high setting.

3 Put all the ingredients for the kebabs into a bowl and mix by hand until everything is evenly combined.

4 With wet hands, form the mixture into sausage shapes around 12 metal skewers, squeezing and pressing so that the meat holds together and sticks to the skewers.

5 Put the skewers on the rack of the grill pan and grill for 4–5 minutes until well browned, then turn them over carefully and grill for another 4–5 minutes to brown the other side. Serve hot, with the sauce.

Sabrina Ghayour

an arabian mezze platter

HUMMUS
1 x 400g can chickpeas
1 large clove garlic, crushed to a paste
    with a little salt
about 3 tbsp olive oil
juice of 1–2 lemons, to taste
2–4 tbsp tahini (sesame seed paste)
paprika and warm pitta bread, to serve

PIQUILLO PEPPER AND FETA ROLLS
1 x 220g jar Spanish piquillo peppers
175g feta cheese
2 tbsp finely chopped fresh mint
extra virgin olive oil
lemon juice
1–2 tbsp full-fat Greek yoghurt (optional)
1 tbsp pine nuts, roughly chopped

In Middle Eastern culture, food is made for sharing with others and variety is the key to enjoyment of every meal. The word 'mezze' means 'to taste' and my trio of Arabian-style mezze allows guests to do exactly that. Everyone loves hummus and you can't beat a homemade recipe — once you try it, there is no going back. The roasted sweet red peppers are perfectly complemented by the salty feta cheese filling with cooling fresh mint and a zing of lemon juice. The aubergine chermoula is rich and moreish, bursting with sweet and savoury flavours. This kind of starter always wins people over as there is something to suit everyone's tastes — just make sure you make enough, as people always ask for seconds!

Hummus

1 Drain the chickpeas, reserving the brine. Using a mortar and pestle, mash the chickpeas by hand to get a nice rough texture, using about 2 tbsp of the brine to help the process. Add the garlic and 2 tbsp of the olive oil and keep mashing to combine together with the chickpeas.

2 Now gradually add the lemon juice and tahini, mixing thoroughly after each addition and tasting as you go to get the flavour and consistency you like. Add salt and pepper at the end.

3 Transfer to a serving bowl, drizzle the remaining 1 tbsp olive oil over the top and sprinkle with paprika for colour. Cover and refrigerate until serving time. Serve with warm pitta bread for dipping.

Piquillo pepper and feta rolls

1 Drain the peppers and pat them with kitchen paper to remove excess oil and make them easier to handle. Lay them on a board and carefully open them out flat, making a lengthways slit in the flesh if necessary. Scrape off and discard any stray seeds and black skin.

AUBERGINE CHERMOULA

5 tbsp olive oil

1 large aubergine, peeled and cut into
   2.5cm cubes

1 onion, sliced thinly into half moons

3 cloves garlic, crushed to a paste with
   a little salt

½ tsp ground cumin

1 tsp sweet paprika

½ red pepper, cut lengthways into thin
   strips and halved

handful of plump golden raisins

300g ripe tomatoes, chopped

3 tbsp red wine vinegar

2 tsp caster sugar

1 tbsp chilli and tomato jam (to thicken
   and enrich the mix)

4–6 slices toasted ciabatta drizzled with
   olive oil, to serve

2 Mash the feta in a bowl with a fork. Add the mint, a good drizzle of olive oil and a squeeze or two of lemon juice. Mix well, slacken with a little yoghurt if necessary, then add the pine nuts and pepper to taste.

3 Place about 2 tsp of the cheese mixture in the centre of each pepper (there are usually about 12 in a jar) then roll the pepper around the cheese. The pepper will stick to the cheese and not require anything else to keep it in place.

Aubergine chermoula

1 Heat the oil in a saucepan on medium heat until hot. Add the aubergine and sauté for 6–8 minutes until golden brown, seasoning with a little salt halfway through. Remove from the pan and set aside.

2 Put the onion in the pan and cook on low heat for about 5 minutes, stirring occasionally. Just as the onion starts to brown, stir in the garlic, cumin and paprika, then add the red pepper strips and sauté for a few minutes. Now add the raisins and fry for 5 minutes more before stirring in the tomatoes. Cook for 5 minutes on medium heat until the tomatoes are softened before adding the vinegar, sugar and chilli and tomato jam.

3 Increase the heat and stir-fry the mix for a few minutes without letting it burn, then turn the heat right down, tip in the aubergine and lightly mash the mixture for a few minutes to ensure it is all even. Taste for seasoning and serve at room temperature, with the ciabatta.

Cathy Shilling

tapas

CHORIZO EN JEREZ
8 small chorizo cooking sausages (about
    20g each), sliced into 1cm-thick coins
about 150ml amontillado sherry

PIMIENTOS DE PADRON
2 tbsp olive oil
12–16 pimientos de Padron
sea salt

GAMBAS CON AJO
50g butter
3–5 cloves garlic, finely sliced
1 small hot red chilli, deseeded and finely
    chopped
12 uncooked prawns, peeled with tails
    left on
handful of fresh flat-leaf parsley,
    leaves chopped

PAN CON TOMATE
4 ripe tomatoes, roughly chopped
olive oil
1–2 tsp caster sugar – depending on
    the sweetness of the tomatoes
1 clove garlic, halved (optional)
1 thin baguette, cut into 1cm-thick slices
handful of fresh basil leaves, torn

DATILES CON BACON
6 thin rashers streaky bacon
12 dates, pitted
12 cocktail sticks

SERVES FOUR TO SIX

These gorgeous little creations are simple to make yet very *delicioso*, and all authentic from España! Take time to arrange the dishes to create a stunning, visually appetizing starter. I thoroughly recommend buying uncooked chorizo, as it really soaks up the sherry. Serve with pieces of Manchego cheese, Serrano ham and olives to complement the fabulous array of tapas.

Chorizo en jerez

Preheat the oven to 190°C/Gas 5. Place the chorizo slices in an ovenproof dish and pour over enough sherry to cover them. Bake for 15 minutes and drain before serving.

Pimientos de Padron

Heat the oil in a large frying pan until hot. Add the peppers and cook for 2–3 minutes on medium heat, turning constantly, until just blistering on the skin. Transfer to a bowl with a slotted spoon and sprinkle with lots of sea salt.

Gambas con ajo

Melt the butter in a frying pan until foaming. Add the garlic and chilli and fry on low heat for 1–2 minutes, stirring constantly to prevent browning. Add the prawns, increase the heat to medium and cook for a few minutes until they turn a gorgeous flamingo pink colour. Season with salt and pepper and serve sprinkled with parsley.

Pan con tomate

Blitz the tomatoes to a purée in a food processor. Tip the purée into a sieve set over a bowl and stir in a dash of olive oil with sugar, salt and pepper to taste. Leave to stand for a couple of hours to drain the excess water off the purée. Rub the bread with the cut-sides of the garlic clove (if using), then brush both sides of the bread with olive oil and grill until golden on both sides. Put a good spreading of the tomato purée from the sieve on each piece of toast, drizzle with olive oil and top with basil.

Datiles con bacon

Preheat the oven to 190°C/Gas 5. Cut each bacon rasher in half and wrap tightly around each date. Place in an ovenproof dish and bake for about 30 minutes until the bacon is just about to crisp. Serve with cocktail sticks.

Chris Bush

tea-smoked chicken salad

3 skinless, boneless chicken breasts
about 500ml chicken stock
100g loose-leaf tea
100g dark soft brown sugar

FOR THE PULSES

60g dried yellow split peas, soaked in cold
    water overnight
60g dried green lentils
1 onion, chopped
1 unwaxed lemon, sliced
2 bay leaves
a few sprigs each fresh thyme and marjoram

FOR THE DRESSING

2 tbsp cold-pressed rapeseed oil (this has
    a nutty taste) or oil of your choice
2 tsp red wine vinegar
1 tbsp chopped fresh mint
1 tsp chopped fresh marjoram
1 rounded tsp wholegrain mustard
½ lemon

TO SERVE

1 x 110g bag mixed watercress, spinach
    and rocket
25g chopped walnuts, to garnish
edible flowers, to decorate (optional)

SERVES FOUR

This is a highly unusual but truly delicious salad: tea-smoking gives a taste quite unlike any other. It will, however, entirely fug up your kitchen, so if you have an outdoor wood-burner or barbeque, that's all the better.

1 Place the chicken breasts between 2 sheets of clingfilm and pound with a rolling pin until about 1cm thick. Put the chicken into a large frying pan (or 2 smaller pans) and add enough stock to cover. Bring to the boil, turn down the heat and poach until the chicken is just cooked, about 5 minutes.

2 To smoke the chicken, make sure your kitchen is well ventilated and have the extractor fan going. Double line a wok with foil. Mix the tea and sugar together and tip into the wok. Place a metal rack over the wok (a circular cake rack is ideal) and put the chicken pieces on the rack. Now place the wok on medium heat and heat until you see small curls of smoke. Cover with a tight-fitting lid, or use any lid that partially fits and a large sheet of foil to keep the smoke in. Leave the wok on low to medium heat for about 20 minutes until the chicken is tinged golden brown (during this time the tea should be sending up curls of smoke, not clouds). Now turn off the heat and leave the wok covered until it is completely cool. Set aside, covered, until needed.

3 Prepare the pulses. Drain and rinse the split peas, and rinse the lentils. Place in separate saucepans and cover generously with cold water. Divide the onion, lemon slices, bay leaves and herb sprigs between the 2 pans and bring them both to the boil. Half cover the pans and simmer until the pulses are tender. The lentils will take around 45 minutes and the split peas up to 2 hours.

4 Meanwhile, make the dressing by whisking together the oil, vinegar, mint, marjoram and mustard. Add a squeeze of lemon juice and salt and pepper to taste.

5 Drain the pulses and stir the dressing through them while they are hot. Allow them to cool and absorb the dressing.

6 To serve, fold the salad leaves through the pulses and divide between 4 bowls or plates. Shred the chicken and add to the salad. Garnish with chopped walnuts — and edible flowers if you like.

Natalie Carter

seared fillet of beef with sweet romano peppers

50g couscous
100ml boiling water
3 Romano peppers, halved lengthways
    and deseeded, keeping the stalks on
olive oil
100g feta cheese
2 tbsp chopped fresh basil
6 cherry vine tomatoes, finely chopped
1 plump clove garlic, finely chopped
2 tsp chopped fresh oregano
1½ tbsp mayonnaise
1½ tbsp full-fat soft cheese
75g pecorino cheese
3 x 175g fillet steaks

SERVES SIX

I chose this dish since fillet of beef is the tastiest and most tender cut of beef you can have. I love fillet of beef lightly seared to lock in the juices of the meat whilst giving a lightly chargrilled taste. The peppers are roasted and filled with a mix of garlic, chopped vine tomatoes, cheese and couscous to add an interesting twist. This is the perfect dish to serve on a balmy summer's evening, with a glass of sparkling wine or a medium-dry white such as Sauvignon Blanc. The dish is light so you don't have to worry about your summer figure, yet is still filling and laced with flavour! *Viva la dieta mediterranea!*

1 Put the couscous into a bowl and pour in the boiling water. Stir, then cover and leave until the couscous is softened and the water absorbed – about 10 minutes.

2 Meanwhile, preheat the grill on medium-high setting. Brush the skin of the pepper halves lightly with olive oil and grill skin-side up for 8–10 minutes until the skins soften slightly. Remove the peppers from the grill and leave the grill on.

3 Fluff up the couscous with a fork, crumble in the feta and add the basil, tomatoes, garlic and oregano with plenty of black pepper and salt if needed. Fork through gently.

4 Turn the peppers over so that they are skin-side down and spoon the couscous mixture into them. Mix the mayonnaise and soft cheese together and spoon over the couscous to cover, then grate the pecorino on top. Grill for about 3 minutes or until the cheese has melted. Keep warm.

5 Heat a griddle pan until hot. Brush the steaks with olive oil and season with salt and pepper. Place the steaks in the pan and sear on medium to high heat for 2 minutes on each side. Remove from the heat and leave to rest for 5 minutes, then cut into thin slices on the diagonal.

6 Divide the steak slices between 6 plates and place 1 stuffed pepper half alongside. Serve immediately, while still warm.

Phil Davies

roasted red pepper soup with homemade pesto

7 red peppers, halved, cored and deseeded
olive oil
2 onions, chopped
200g potato, peeled and diced
1 small chilli, deseeded and finely chopped
1 clove garlic, crushed
1 tsp chopped fresh thyme
1 x 400g can tomatoes
2 tbsp tomato purée
2 litres vegetable stock
2 tsp chopped fresh flat-leaf parsley
½ tsp dried oregano
handful of fresh basil leaves

FOR THE PESTO
3 cloves garlic, roughly chopped
1 tsp rock salt
25g pine nuts, toasted
1 large bunch fresh basil, leaves torn
50g Parmesan cheese, freshly grated
100–125ml extra virgin olive oil

SERVES EIGHT

Don't even think about taking short cuts with this one! The grilling of the peppers until they're absolutely blackened really creates a unique flavour. It's a bit messy peeling the burnt skins off, but have faith – it's worth it to uncover the seductively sweet flesh beneath. After that it's a simple assembly job, all rounded off with fresh Italian herb bread. A real taste of the Med!

1 Preheat the grill on its highest setting. Lay the peppers skin-side up in a large baking tray and rub olive oil all over the skins. Grill for 15–20 minutes until well charred, then remove and place in a plastic bag to cool.

2 Meanwhile, make the pesto. Pound the garlic and salt to a pulp with a mortar and pestle. Add the pine nuts as the garlic breaks down, then work in the basil. Mix in the Parmesan and then the olive oil and pound to a textured paste. (If you prefer to use a food processor to make this quicker, first blitz the garlic, pine nuts, cheese and basil, then slowly pour in the oil with the machine running.) Cover and set aside until needed.

3 Now continue with the soup. Heat 2 tbsp olive oil in a large saucepan, add the onions and fry on low heat, stirring occasionally, for 10 minutes or until soft but not coloured. Add the potato, chilli, garlic and thyme and continue to fry until the onions start to brown. Add the tomatoes and tomato purée with seasoning to taste and simmer for about 10 minutes.

4 Meanwhile, remove and discard the loosened pepper skins. Tear the flesh and chop into rough pieces.

5 Add the peppers to the pan with the stock, parsley, oregano and half the basil (keep the small leaves back for garnish). Simmer gently for 10 minutes without boiling, then remove from the heat and leave to cool a little before blending in batches until smooth. Taste for seasoning.

6 Serve hot in 8 warmed bowls, each one swirled with pesto and garnished with the reserved small basil leaves.

Jon Revell

cured salmon with beetroot & red onion salad

2 tbsp mustard seeds
1½ tsp caraway seeds
1 tbsp green peppercorns
1 x 20cm side of salmon (weighing about 480g), skinned
2 tbsp finely chopped fresh dill
finely grated zest of 1 unwaxed lemon
3 tbsp sea salt

FOR THE SALAD
1 red onion, sliced into thin half-moon shapes
juice of 1 lemon
2 uncooked beetroot (about 350g total weight)

TO SERVE
large handful of salad leaves
2 spring onions, thinly sliced
extra virgin olive oil

SERVES SIX TO EIGHT

This is an incredibly easy starter which can be done well ahead of time and looks impressive when, as I like to amuse myself by doing, it is arranged like a 1950s first-class airline meal.

1 Grind the mustard and caraway seeds with the peppercorns in a mortar and pestle, then spread over the flesh side of the salmon. Sprinkle over the dill, lemon zest and salt, then press firmly so that they adhere to the fish. Wrap the fish tightly in clingfilm and refrigerate for 24 hours.

2 Prepare the salad. Place the onion slices in a bowl with the lemon juice and leave to marinate for about 2 hours. Meanwhile, lower the beetroot into a saucepan of boiling water and bring back to the boil. Cover and simmer for 1¼–1½ hours until the beetroot are tender. Drain and leave until cool enough to handle, then peel and chop. Mix the beetroot with the marinated onion and season well with salt and pepper.

3 To serve, divide the beetroot and onion between 6–8 plates. Slice the salmon thinly and place on top, then garnish with the salad leaves and spring onions. Drizzle with a little extra virgin olive oil and finish with a grinding of black pepper.

main courses

Jon Pattullo

vegetable lasagne

4 tbsp chilli oil, or 2 tbsp chilli oil and
  2 tbsp olive oil
1 red onion, thinly sliced
2 courgettes, thinly sliced
2 red peppers, cored, deseeded and
  thinly sliced
2 aubergines, cut into 1cm-thick slices
1 x 350g tub ready-made béchamel or
  cheese sauce
6 fresh lasagne sheets
75g Parmesan cheese, freshly grated

SERVES FOUR

I wanted to do a vegetable lasagne using these vegetables to make the dish sturdier than the sloppy versions I have experienced before. I chose to use aubergine as the main ingredient as it retains its shape well. Red onion was used since it has a superior flavour and gives the dish crunch and texture, and the red peppers give the dish a good flavour once all the vegetables have been cooked together in the chilli oil. Vegetarian food can be ignored or glossed over but I wanted to create a dish that I was proud of.

1 Heat 2 tbsp chilli oil in a large frying pan until hot and fry the onion, courgettes and red peppers on low to medium heat for about 20 minutes until soft. Remove with a slotted spoon and set aside.

2 Add half the aubergine slices to the pan and fry for about 5 minutes on each side until evenly browned. Remove and repeat with the remaining aubergine slices, adding more chilli oil as necessary (or use olive oil for a milder flavour).

Preheat the oven to 200°C/Gas 6.

4 Spread a little of the béchamel or cheese sauce over the bottom of a 30 x 20cm baking dish. Place 2 lasagne sheets side by side in the dish, then scatter over half the courgette and pepper mix and one-third of the Parmesan. Repeat the layers, then top with the remaining 2 lasagne sheets.

5 Lay the slices of aubergine on the lasagne, overlapping them slightly if necessary. Coat with the remaining béchamel or cheese sauce and sprinkle over the remaining Parmesan.

6 Bake for 40–45 minutes or until the top is golden and bubbling. Leave to rest for 5 minutes before serving.

Kelly Hatt

best end of lamb with fresh herbs, parmesan crust & red wine sauce

2 best ends of lamb with 6–7 ribs each,
   boned by your butcher
3 tbsp olive oil
4 heaped tbsp finely chopped fresh herbs –
   I would recommend a mix of basil,
   rosemary, parsley and coriander
40g grated Parmesan cheese
40g fresh white breadcrumbs

FOR THE SAUCE
1 tbsp olive oil
3 shallots, finely chopped
400ml red wine
1 tbsp caster sugar, or more to taste
splash of balsamic vinegar

Lamb is my favourite, and the key to this dish is the quality of the meat. I developed this recipe in conjunction with my butcher, Michael. A good-quality butcher will always be happy to discuss different cuts of meat and prepare them for you. Both the Parmesan crust and the richness of the red wine sauce complement the lamb perfectly. This works equally well for a dinner party or as a twist on your traditional Sunday roast. Serve with garlic mash and green beans.

1 Preheat the oven to 200°C/Gas 6.

2 Brush the inside of each best end with 1 tbsp olive oil, season with salt and pepper and cover with the herbs. Roll each piece up to form a sausage shape, wrapping the flap of fat around the eye of the meat, and secure with several wooden cocktail sticks. Season the outside of the lamb and brush with the remaining olive oil, then coat with the grated Parmesan and breadcrumbs.

3 Place the joints on a roasting tray and roast for 25–30 minutes for rare to medium-rare meat, 35 minutes for medium.

4 Meanwhile, make the sauce. Heat the olive oil in a frying pan and cook the shallots on low heat for 5–8 minutes until soft. Add the wine and sugar, stir well and boil to reduce by half. Now add the balsamic vinegar and taste the sauce – it should be sweet and syrupy. If necessary, add a little more sugar.

5 Remove the lamb from the oven and leave to rest in a warm place for 10 minutes before cutting each joint into 9 slices. Pour any juices from the meat into the sauce and taste for seasoning.

6 Arrange 3 slices of lamb on each of 6 warmed plates and drizzle over the sauce. Serve straightaway.

Zac Turner

chicken à la zac

4 large skinless, boneless chicken breasts
  – I buy corn-fed and free range
8 rashers back bacon (preferably dry-cure),
  trimmed of excess fat
300g young spinach leaves, well washed
75g sun-blushed or sun-drenched tomatoes,
  drained and chopped
1 x 400g can cannellini beans, drained
  and rinsed
200ml chicken stock
1 onion, finely chopped
1 clove garlic, finely chopped

FOR THE MARINADE
4 tbsp extra virgin olive oil
1 medium-hot red chilli, finely chopped
  (with or without seeds according to taste)
3 cloves garlic, crushed
handful of fresh basil leaves, torn

FOR THE CARROT AND SWEDE TOWERS
300g carrots, peeled and cut into chunks
300g swede, peeled and cut into chunks
knob of butter, softened, plus extra for greasing
4 tbsp double cream

SERVES FOUR

It's really important to wrap the bacon tightly round the chicken, but it isn't the easiest thing. The chicken breasts aren't the most aesthetically pleasing thing when they're prepped, but once they're cooked, they're lovely.

1 Butterfly each chicken breast: make a slit along the length of the thinnest side of the meat with a sharp knife, then cut through the flesh to the other side and open the breast out flat. Place the breasts in a large, shallow ovenproof dish with the bacon.

2 Whisk the marinade ingredients together with black pepper to taste, pour over the chicken and bacon and massage well into the meat. Cover and leave to marinate in the fridge for at least 6 hours or overnight.

3 Place the wet spinach in a large saucepan with a sprinkling of salt. Cover and cook on medium heat for 5 minutes or until wilted, shaking the pan frequently. Drain well and squeeze out as much water as possible, then chop finely and leave until cold.

4 Meanwhile, place the carrots and swedes in a pan of cold salted water, cover and bring to the boil, then boil for about 20 minutes until they are soft. Drain, return to the pan and dry out on low heat before mashing and beating in the butter and cream. Season to taste.

5 Preheat the oven to 190°C/Gas 5. Stand 4 metal chefs' rings (or four 7 x 5cm plain pastry cutters) on a baking sheet. Brush the insides with butter and fill with the mash.

6 Mix the spinach with the tomatoes and salt and pepper to taste. Lay the chicken breasts on a board with their cut sides uppermost and divide the spinach mixture equally between them. Fold the chicken over to enclose the filling, then wrap each breast tightly in 2 bacon rashers.

7 Tip the cannellini beans into the marinating dish, add the stock, onion and garlic and mix well. Place the chicken on the bed of beans and roast for 40 minutes, turning the breasts over halfway and putting the vegetable towers in the oven for the last 10 minutes to heat through.

8 Leave the chicken to rest in a warm place for 5 minutes, then cut into thick slices on the diagonal. Remove the rings from the mash and place the towers on 4 warmed plates with the chicken and beans. Serve straightaway.

William Henry

chicken marsala with herbed green beans

5 skinless, boneless chicken breasts
2–3 tbsp plain flour
3 tbsp olive oil
200ml Marsala wine
large knob of butter
freshly cooked pasta, such as tagliatelle,
    to serve

FOR THE BEANS
400g French beans, topped and tailed
3 tbsp olive oil
2 tbsp chopped fresh mint
1 clove garlic, finely chopped

SERVES FIVE

With this main I wanted to mix hot and cold: the beans had been marinated for 6 hours and kept cool, and were only served at the last minute to complement the hot chicken. Make sure you don't put too much flour over the chicken as this makes the sauce too thick and gooey.

1 Plunge the beans into a saucepan of boiling salted water. Quickly bring back to the boil, then simmer until the beans are al dente, about 8 minutes. Drain the beans well, tip into a bowl and toss with the olive oil, mint, garlic and seasoning to taste. Cool, then cover and keep in the fridge until serving time.

2 Flatten each chicken breast between 2 sheets of clingfilm by pounding with a meat mallet, rolling pin or the base of a saucepan. Take care not to tear the flesh. Cut each breast in half – this will make them easier to cook.

3 Spread the flour out on a tray and season with salt and pepper. Toss the chicken in the flour until lightly and evenly coated, shaking off the excess.

4 Heat the olive oil in a large frying pan on medium to high heat until hot. Place half the chicken in the pan and cook for 5 minutes or until golden brown on both sides, turning halfway. Remove and keep warm while frying the remaining chicken.

5 Pour the Marsala into the pan and increase the heat to high. Allow to bubble and reduce slightly, stirring vigorously and scraping up the bits from the bottom of the pan. Now add the butter and seasoning to taste and stir until the butter has melted into the sauce. Return all the chicken pieces to the pan and heat through for 2 minutes, spooning the sauce over the meat.

6 Divide the beans and chicken between 5 warmed plates. Pour the sauce over the chicken and serve straightaway – with pasta of your choice.

Bindi Holding

tangy tomato & fish curry

800g large vine tomatoes – nice and ripe
24 cherry tomatoes
2 tsp mustard seeds
2 tsp cumin seeds
1 dried red chilli
2 tbsp vegetable oil
1 tsp turmeric
1 tsp ground coriander
1 tsp ground cumin
½ tsp chilli powder – as hot as you like
½ tsp asafoetida
large knob of fresh root ginger, finely chopped
2 cloves garlic, chopped, sliced or crushed –
    whatever you like
1 tsp salt
2 tsp lemon juice, or to taste
1 tsp caster sugar, or to taste
600–700g skinless white fish fillets, cut into
    20 chunks
large knob of butter, softened
handful of fresh coriander leaves, chopped

SERVES FOUR

With fusion cooking being all the rage these days, I decided to get in on the act. This scrumptious marriage of firm, white flesh with evocative hints of spice and a tangy tomato sauce creates a perfect year-round curry for all occasions.

1 You can leave the tomatoes unpeeled if you like, and fish out the skins before serving, but if you prefer to start with them peeled, this is how you do it. Score a cross in the bottom of each tomato. Put a quarter of the tomatoes into a large heatproof bowl and cover with boiling water. Leave for about 30 seconds, just until the skins start to peel back, then lift the tomatoes out with a slotted spoon and plunge into a bowl of cold water. Drain, then peel off the skins with your fingers. Repeat with the remaining tomatoes, then cut into quarters and remove any hard white cores.

2 Put the mustard and cumin seeds into a non-stick frying pan with the dried chilli. Dry-fry on medium heat for a few minutes, stirring frequently, until the seeds pop, then grind to a powder using a mortar and pestle.

3 Heat the oil in a flameproof casserole or large saucepan on medium heat until hot. Tip in the spice powder with all the other spices and the asafoetida. Stir to mix with the oil, then add the ginger and garlic and soften for a few minutes, stirring occasionally.

4 Add the tomatoes and salt, then add lemon juice, sugar and pepper to taste. Toss to mix, cover the pan and simmer on low to medium heat for about 30 minutes, stirring and pressing the tomatoes frequently, until they have cooked into a ragù. Remove from the heat and leave to cool (the flavour will improve if the curry is left overnight in the fridge).

5 When you are ready to serve, reheat the ragù until bubbling and stir in a splash or two of hot water if the consistency is too thick. Taste for seasoning and add more lemon juice and sugar if you like.

6 Now add the fish, making sure it is immersed in the ragù. Cover and simmer gently for 5 minutes or just until the fish is cooked. Turn off the heat and add the butter to glaze. Leave to stand for 5 minutes and sprinkle with the coriander before serving.

Jilly Fitzgerald

imam bayildi with rosemary-roasted potatoes

600g slim aubergines, cut into slices about 8mm thick (ends discarded)
1 x 400g can tomatoes
about 150ml olive oil
1 onion, finely chopped
1 tsp dried oregano
1 tsp dried thyme
1 tsp caster sugar
85g butter
85g plain flour
600ml milk
85g Parmesan cheese, freshly grated
2 medium egg yolks
1–2 tbsp chopped fresh flat-leaf parsley

FOR THE POTATOES
1kg floury potatoes (such as King Edward or Maris Piper), peeled and cut into chunks
75g butter
juice of 1 lemon
5–6 sprigs fresh rosemary
about 150ml hot water

SERVES SIX

This is always a hit with family and friends. The original was topped simply with grated cheese but, entertaining a vegetarian guest, I felt something a little more substantial was needed and topped the bake with a moussaka crust to make it more gutsy and wholesome.

1 Immerse the aubergine slices in a bowl of cold salted water. Leave to soak for 30 minutes, then rinse and squeeze gently. Leave to drain and dry in a large sieve or colander for another 30 minutes.

2 Meanwhile, make a tomato sauce. Whiz the canned tomatoes to a purée in a blender, then tip into a saucepan and add 2 tbsp olive oil, the onion, herbs, sugar and seasoning to taste. Bring to the boil, cover and simmer on very low heat for 40–45 minutes, stirring occasionally.

3 Now fry the aubergine slices in hot olive oil until golden brown on both sides. This needs to be done in batches in a large frying pan and should take about 8 minutes for each batch. As each batch is fried, remove the slices from the pan and drain on kitchen paper.

4 Preheat the oven to 190°C/Gas 5.

5 Put the potatoes into a large roasting tin. Melt the butter in a small pan and pour over the potatoes. Add the lemon juice, rosemary and seasoning and stir until the potatoes are glossy. Pour 150ml hot water into one end of the tin and roast for 1¼ hours or until the potatoes are golden, basting halfway and adding a little more water if needed.

6 Meanwhile, make a cheese sauce. Melt the butter in a saucepan on medium heat, add the flour and stir to form a roux. Cook for 1 minute, stirring, then remove from the heat and gradually add the milk, whisking vigorously after each addition. Return to the heat and bring to the boil, stirring, then simmer for about 2 minutes until thickened and smooth. Remove from the heat and cool slightly, then stir in 30g of the Parmesan and the egg yolks.

7 Arrange half the aubergine slices over the bottom of a 25 x 18 x 6.5cm baking dish. Spread the tomato sauce on top, then cover with the remaining aubergines followed by the cheese sauce and remaining Parmesan. Bake for 25–30 minutes or until golden. Leave to rest for 5–10 minutes before serving with the potatoes.

Hayley Williams

monkfish with mediterranean salsa & lemon mash

finely grated zest of 3 unwaxed lemons
2 sprigs fresh rosemary, needles finely chopped
4 pieces monkfish fillet (about 150g each)
8 thin slices Parma ham
olive oil

FOR THE SALSA
100g black olives, pitted and finely chopped
50g green olives, pitted and finely chopped
1 red chilli, finely chopped (with or without
    seeds according to taste)
handful of mixed fresh herb leaves (such as
    basil, marjoram and parsley), chopped
1 small celery heart, finely chopped
2 cloves garlic (more if you like), finely
    chopped or crushed
juice of 2 lemons
3–4 tbsp extra virgin olive oil
balsamic vinegar, to taste

FOR THE MASH
900g floury potatoes (such as Maris Piper or
    King Edward), peeled and cut into chunks
50g butter, softened
4 tbsp extra virgin olive oil
juice of 1 lemon
about 100ml hot milk

SERVES FOUR

Monkfish is brilliant for guests who don't like fishy fish as it's more like a steak. The fluffy lemon mash is thankfully quite subtle since it needs to take on the almighty flavoursome salsa (the more garlic the better). I tend to slice the monkfish and place it on the mash potato, then scatter the salsa around it to give a fabulous restaurant look. You must, must try it.

1 Mix the lemon zest and rosemary together with black pepper to taste, then rub all over the fish. Wrap each piece of fish in 2 slices of Parma ham and place on a roasting tray. Keep in the fridge while you make the salsa and mash.

2 For the salsa, mix all the chopped ingredients in a large bowl with the lemon juice, then add olive oil, balsamic vinegar and salt and pepper to taste. Cover and refrigerate until serving time.

3 For the mash, put the potatoes into a large saucepan of cold salted water, cover and bring to the boil on high heat. Lower the heat to medium and simmer for 15–20 minutes until the potatoes are tender. Drain the potatoes and return to the pan to dry out on low heat for a minute or two, then remove from the heat and mash until smooth. Beat in the butter, olive oil and lemon juice, adding salt and pepper to taste. Set aside.

4 Preheat the oven to 220°C/Gas 7. Remove the fish from the fridge.

5 Drizzle the fish with olive oil, place the tray in the oven and roast for 10–12 minutes. Remove from the oven and leave to rest for 5 minutes. Meanwhile, reheat the mash with the hot milk, beating vigorously.

6 Serve the fish with the mash, with spoonfuls of salsa on the side.

Natalie Morrison

lamb tagine with romero peppers & fragrant couscous

750g boneless shoulder of lamb, diced
3 tbsp harissa paste
olive oil
1 large onion, roughly chopped
1 x 250g punnet vine tomatoes, roughly
   chopped
5 cloves garlic, roughly chopped
1 tbsp grated fresh root ginger
1 tsp paprika
½ tsp ground cinnamon
1 tbsp runny honey
175ml red wine
300ml lamb or chicken stock
200g fine green beans, trimmed and halved
1 x 420g can butter beans, drained and rinsed

FOR THE PEPPERS AND COUSCOUS
3 Romero or Romano peppers, halved
   lengthways, cored and deseeded
3 tbsp olive oil, plus extra for drizzling
200g couscous
225ml hot vegetable stock
3 tbsp chopped fresh flat-leaf parsley
4 tbsp chopped fresh coriander

TO SERVE
1 x 150g carton plain yoghurt
2 tbsp finely chopped fresh mint

SERVES SIX

This is quite a spicy dish, but I serve it with a mint yoghurt to help cool it down. I use a shop-bought jar of harissa paste – you can make it yourself, but why would you when someone else wants to make it for you?

1 Put the lamb into a large bowl and coat with the harissa paste. Heat a glug of olive oil in a large flameproof casserole or saucepan until hot. Add the lamb in batches and fry on medium to high heat until browned on all sides, then lift on to a plate with a slotted spoon.

2 Add the onion to the pan with a little more olive oil and fry on medium heat for about 5 minutes until soft and golden brown. Add the tomatoes and soften for 2 minutes. Now add the garlic, ginger, paprika, cinnamon and honey and cook together, stirring, for a few minutes.

3 Return the lamb and juices to the pan, pour in the wine and stock and season with salt and pepper to taste. Cover the pan and simmer very gently for 1¾ hours or until the lamb is tender, adding the green beans 10 minutes before the end of cooking and the butter beans for the final 2–3 minutes.

4 While the lamb is cooking, preheat the oven to 200°C/ Gas 6. Line a baking tray with foil.

5 Rub the peppers all over with 1 tbsp olive oil, season with salt and pepper and place them skin-side up on the tray. Place in the oven and roast for 25 minutes or until they are tender.

6 Meanwhile, put the couscous into a large bowl, pour in the stock and stir. Cover and leave to stand for about 10 minutes until the couscous has absorbed the stock. Now fluff up the grains with a fork and add the remaining 2 tbsp olive oil with the parsley, coriander and seasoning to taste. Fork through to mix, cover and set aside.

7 Blend the yoghurt and mint together in a serving bowl with salt and pepper to taste.

8 To serve, transfer the lamb and sauce to a warmed tagine pot if you have one. Place a pepper half skin-side down on each of 6 warmed plates, spoon some couscous into them and drizzle with olive oil. Hand the remaining couscous round in a bowl, together with the bowl of yoghurt and mint.

desserts

Veronica O'Connor

pavlova with summer berries & cream

3 large egg whites
175g caster sugar
1 rounded tsp cornflour
½ tsp malt vinegar
½ tsp vanilla extract

FOR THE TOPPING
200ml double or whipping cream
300g mixed summer berries
icing sugar, to serve

SERVES SIX

People often think meringues are a bit of a mystery. However, this dessert looks impressive but is deceptively simple to make. Serve it to your guests at the table so they can admire your culinary prowess before they go and spoil it all by demolishing it.

1 Preheat the oven to 230°C/Gas 8. Cover a large baking sheet with non-stick baking parchment.

2 Using an electric mixer, beat the egg whites in a large bowl until stiff. Gradually beat in the sugar, maintaining the stiffness, then beat in the remaining ingredients. The meringue should look glossy and be able to keep its shape.

3 Spoon the meringue on to the lined baking sheet and swirl it into a 20–23cm disc shape with a slight dip in the centre. Place in the oven and immediately lower the temperature to 120°C/Gas ½. Bake the pavlova for 1 hour, then turn the oven off, leaving the pavlova inside for another hour or until completely cold (it can be left in the oven overnight).

4 To serve, carefully peel the paper off the pavlova and place the pavlova on a serving plate. Whip the cream until it holds its shape, spread over the pavlova and pile the fruit on top. Sift icing sugar over the fruit at the last moment.

Chris Bush

chocolate brownies with caramel swirls & berry cream

250g dark chocolate, broken into squares
250g butter, cut into cubes
4 medium eggs
325g caster sugar
1 tsp vanilla extract
150g plain flour
pinch of salt

FOR THE BERRY CREAM
200ml mascarpone
100ml double cream
handful each raspberries, blackberries,
    blueberries and strawberries

FOR THE CARAMEL SWIRLS
200g caster sugar

These brownies are of the dense, sticky, fudgy variety but should still have a crisp top. If you're making them in advance, put them somewhere cool (even in the fridge) to firm up but serve at room temperature. The caramel swirls look fancy but are easily done, and provide a wonderful interplay of textures.

1 Make the berry cream. Beat the mascarpone and cream together in a large bowl until evenly blended and thick. Set aside a few whole berries for serving, then hull and chop or slice the strawberries and add to the bowl of cream with the remaining berries. Fold together gently, cover and chill in the fridge until ready to serve.

2 Make the caramel swirls. Place sheets of greaseproof paper flat on your work surface, or grease 2 large baking trays. Put the sugar into a heavy pan and melt slowly on low heat, then cook on high heat, without stirring, until it turns to a rich caramel, about 10 minutes. Remove from the heat. Now dip a whisk or spoon into the caramel and swirl it over the greaseproof paper to make decorative shapes. Set aside at room temperature until needed.

3 Preheat the oven to 180°C/Gas 4. Line the bottom and sides of a greased 30 x 20 x 4cm baking tin with greaseproof paper.

4 Make the brownies. Put the chocolate and butter into a heatproof bowl set over a pan of gently simmering water and heat together until melted and smooth, stirring occasionally. Remove the bowl from the pan and leave the chocolate to cool to room temperature.

5 Beat the eggs, sugar and vanilla extract together in a bowl until light and creamy. Beat in the chocolate mixture, followed by the flour and salt. Pour into the prepared tin and bake for 25 minutes or until risen and firm around the edges. Don't overbake – the cake should be not quite set in the centre. Remove from the oven and leave to cool in the tin.

6 To serve, turn the cake out and cut into 12 squares. Place 1 brownie on each plate and top with a spoonful of berry cream. Decorate with the reserved berries and the caramel swirls.

Natalie Carter

white chocolate & coconut terrine with warm berry compote

vegetable oil, for greasing
1 x 200g bar white chocolate, broken into squares
1 x 200g pack full-fat soft cheese
finely grated zest of 2 large unwaxed oranges
150ml double cream
150ml coconut milk (from a can)
100g block creamed coconut, grated
50g caster sugar
8 fresh mint leaves, to decorate

FOR THE COMPOTE
350g mixed berries – strawberries, raspberries, blackberries and blueberries
75g caster sugar

I love white chocolate and cheesecake, so the white chocolate terrine is a combination of the two but without a biscuit base, as desserts after a good meal need to be light rather than heavy and stodgy. As I love a fusion of flavours I decided to grate orange zest and coconut into the dish. This is a melt-in-the-mouth dish which I would recommend for any occasion – especially if you believe that the way to a heart is through the stomach!

1 Lightly grease a 22 x 12 x 6cm loaf tin and line with clingfilm, leaving a generous overhang.

2 Put the chocolate into a heatproof bowl set over a pan of gently simmering water and heat gently until melted and smooth, stirring occasionally. Remove the bowl from the pan and leave the chocolate to cool to room temperature.

3 Meanwhile, put the cheese into a separate bowl with the orange zest, cream and coconut milk and beat together until light and fluffy. Add the grated coconut and the sugar and beat again until evenly mixed.

4 Pour the cooled chocolate into the cream mix and beat again, then pour into the prepared tin. Smooth the surface and cover the top of the terrine with the overhanging clingfilm, then wrap the tin and freeze for 4–6 hours until the terrine is solid.

5 Make the compote up to an hour before serving. Hull and halve or quarter the strawberries, then place in a saucepan with the other berries and the sugar. Heat gently until the sugar has dissolved and the berry juices start to run – about 5 minutes. Remove from the heat and keep warm.

6 About 15 minutes before serving, remove the terrine from the freezer and unwrap. Dip the tin briefly in a bowl of hot water, then turn the terrine out on to a board and peel off the clingfilm. Leave at room temperature for about 15 minutes to soften slightly, then cut into 8 slices and place each slice on a serving dish. Spoon the warm berry compote on top of the terrine and decorate each serving with a mint leaf.

Samira Mohammed Ali

peach delight

4 ripe peaches
150g butter, cut into small cubes
8 tbsp light soft brown sugar
4 scoops vanilla ice cream, to serve

My peach delight is the life and soul of the party. It is not too heavy so you can have a dance after the three-course meal you've just scoffed, as it won't make you feel sluggish. I choose it as it's my signature dinner-party dish which everyone loves. You can't go wrong with my lovely, beautiful, juicy peaches!

1 Preheat the grill on medium setting.

2 Cut the peaches in half and remove the stones. Put the peaches cut-side up on a baking tray and grill for 4–5 minutes or until tinged golden brown.

3 Meanwhile, melt the butter in a pan on low to medium heat and add the sugar. Stir on the heat until the sugar has dissolved and formed a smooth, caramelly sauce.

4 Put 2 peach halves cut-side up on each of 4 plates. Drizzle the sauce over the top and serve with a scoop of ice cream.

Jay Davies

pineapple grilled on an open fire with rum sauce

1 ripe pineapple
vanilla ice cream, to serve

FOR THE SAUCE
2–3 tbsp dark muscovado sugar
2 tsp ground ginger
2 tbsp unsalted butter
2–3 tbsp dark rum

Grilled pineapple is a tropical pudding which is ideal to follow a chargrilled main course. When barbequing, so many people cook a few steaks or sausages and then let the coals burn down. Instead, use the smouldering embers to wow your guests. The heat makes some of the water content of the fruit evaporate and you end up with a sweetened, caramelized warm fruit. The rum sauce creates a Caribbean flavour which is a perfect way to round off an afternoon in the sunshine.

1 Quarter the pineapple lengthways with a sharp knife and cut out any hard white core, then score the flesh in a diamond pattern.

2 Heat the sauce ingredients very gently in a saucepan until the sugar has dissolved, stirring frequently. Brush the sauce over the pineapple flesh, working it into the cuts.

3 Place the pieces of pineapple flesh-side down on the grid of a hot barbeque and cook for about 5 minutes until they become tinged golden brown. Turn them if necessary to make sure all the flesh is cooked. Serve hot with scoops of ice cream, drizzled with any remaining sauce.

Hayley Williams

raspberry & lemon shots

7 raspberry jelly cubes (75g from
   a 135g packet)
150ml boiling water
1 tbsp orange-flavoured liqueur
125g mascarpone
40g icing sugar
2 tsp lemon juice
24 small raspberries

I love visual desserts, so the clean colours of red and white in little shot glasses are the perfect end to a meal. You can add any flavoured liqueur to the jelly but you can't beat the creamy lemon topping; every mouthful results in an 'mmmm'. You can make them in four 200ml glasses if you find it too fiddly in the shot glasses, and sparklers are a must-have decoration for special occasions!

1 Put the cubes of jelly into a measuring jug and pour in the boiling water. Stir until the jelly has dissolved, then make up to 300ml with cold water and stir in the liqueur.

2 Leave the jelly to cool (but not set) before pouring into 8 shot glasses. Chill in the fridge until set, about 4 hours.

3 Put the mascarpone into a bowl, sift in the icing sugar and add the lemon juice. Stir well to mix, then spoon into the shot glasses on top of the set jellies and finish each one with 3 raspberries. Keep in the fridge until you are ready to serve.

John O'Connor

raspberry mousse in chocolate cups & mini trifles

RASPBERRY MOUSSE IN CHOCOLATE CUPS
150g good-quality dark chocolate
200g raspberries
50g golden caster sugar
3 sheets gelatine (5g total weight)
2 tbsp boiling water
2 medium egg whites
1 x 150g carton fat-free natural yoghurt
icing sugar, for dusting

SERVES SIX

For me, choosing a dessert to make for a dinner party can be difficult. Some guests like chocolatey ones, some like fruity ones, and others prefer creamy puddings. This is why I have come up with two small taster desserts which even the fussiest dinner-party guests will love.

Raspberry mousse in chocolate cups

1 Make the chocolate cups (these can be done 1–2 days ahead and kept in a rigid container in the fridge). Melt the chocolate in a bowl set over a pan of gently simmering water. Remove the bowl from the pan and let the chocolate stand for a few minutes to cool but not set. Now pour a good dessertspoonful of the chocolate into a 6.5cm silicone muffin mould and carefully tip the mould at an angle, twisting it round and round so that the chocolate covers the whole of the inside and goes right up to the top edge. Turn the mould upside-down to let the excess chocolate drip back into the bowl, then wipe the top edge clean (this will make the cup easier to remove later). Place in the fridge to harden while you make another 5 chocolate cups. Once these have all hardened, warm the chocolate again very slightly if it is no longer runny enough to use again, and carefully repeat the process to make a double thickness of chocolate inside each mould. Chill in the fridge until this second layer is set, about 20 minutes.

2 For the mousse, reserve 6 raspberries for decoration. Place the remainder in a pan with half the sugar and cook on medium heat for 4–5 minutes, stirring occasionally until the fruit collapses. Tip the cooked fruit into a fine sieve set over a bowl and pass through to deseed. Cool the purée, then chill in the fridge.

3 Soften the sheets of gelatine in a shallow dish of cold water for 4–5 minutes. Lift the sheets out of the water and squeeze to remove excess liquid, then put them into a medium pan. Now add the 2 tbsp boiling water and stir

MINI TRIFLES

½ x 135g packet raspberry jelly, cut into cubes
½ medium sponge flan case (about 65g)
100g raspberries
250g ready-made custard
150ml double or whipping cream
toasted flaked almonds, to decorate

on low to medium heat until the gelatine has completely dissolved – don't let it come to the boil or overcook. Remove the pan from the heat and leave to cool slightly.

4 Meanwhile, whisk the egg whites in a clean bowl with the remaining sugar for 2–3 minutes until stiff peaks form. Place the yoghurt in another bowl and stir in the raspberry purée.

5 Add the yoghurt mix to the dissolved gelatine in the pan. Beat in one-third of the egg whites, then fold in the remainder. Transfer the mousse to a bowl and chill in the fridge for 1–1½ hours or until nearly set.

6 Remove the chocolate cups from the moulds by peeling away the top edges first, then gently peeling off the rest of the mould.

7 To serve, fill the cups with the mousse. Decorate with the reserved raspberries and sift icing sugar over the top.

Mini trifles

1 Dissolve the jelly cubes and make up to 300ml with water according to packet instructions. Leave until cool (but not set).

2 Break up the sponge and divide equally between 6 x 100ml glasses or bowls. Scatter the raspberries over the sponge, then pour over the cooled jelly and press down on the fruit and sponge so that they are submerged. Chill in the fridge for 1½–2 hours, or until the jelly is set.

3 Spoon the custard over the set jelly. Whip the cream to soft peaks and spoon or pipe over the custard. Keep in the fridge until serving time (they will keep well overnight) and sprinkle with toasted flaked almonds before serving.

full-on fancy-dress party; a drinks party with a nod at Halloween but nothing more; or a ghoulish dinner party.

Whichever one you opt for, spell it out in the plainest possible terms. There is nothing worse for your guests than turning up for a house party dressed as Dracula only to discover that everyone else is sipping champagne cocktails in their civvies, with a tealight inside a hollowed-out pumpkin (with the insides used to make the starter, of course) as the only nod to Halloween.

If you're going for full fancy-dress but you're worried that people won't enter into the spirit of things, offer a prize for the best outfit and possibly one for the worst. Send out invites in plenty of time so that guests can sort their outfits, and offer them suggestions for fancy-dress shops in the area. The full-works Halloween party also demands whole-hearted decoration – a bit of fake spider's web and a pumpkin lamp just isn't going to wash with your guests who've paid over the odds for a silly costume and have had to suffer the indignity of wearing it on public transport. The shops are full of Halloween goodies at this time of year, so why not splash out on some novelty paper plates and napkins, along with a giant skull or two?

Drinks: You could go for ghoulish-sounding cocktails, adorned with weird, devilish decoration. But remember, don't sacrifice flavour for presentation – if it tastes as odd as it looks, you'll have some unhappy partygoers on your hands, so test it out first. And nothing can beat a Halloween punch.

Games: The classic one is apple bobbing, but unless your mates are bringing their kids, don't do it. Your female guests won't thank you for encouraging a game that ruins their hair and makes their make-up run. It's probably best to just stick with the food and drink.

Halloween pumpkins: Of course, no party would be complete without a Halloween light. Here are a few tips on how to knock up the perfect one.

- Don't make it too soon before Halloween: remember that pumpkin is a vegetable, so you don't want it to go off. To ensure that it stays fresh for as long as possible, buy one that looks in good shape.
- When cutting a lid, it's best to cut a small bit from the top, rather than slicing a large chunk off. This way you have more pumpkin to play with when you're carving the decoration on the front. Also, don't slice straight across the top otherwise the lid will fall into the pumpkin, but cut at an angle, so that it has a lip to sit on.
- Scrape any flesh from the lid, and do the same for the inside – the more you scoop out the better, so that more light can shine through. Make a particular effort to shape the bottom of the pumpkin, so that your light source has a stable platform.
- Use a soluble marker pen to draw the pattern on the pumpkin before you begin carving it – that way if you cock things up, you can rub it off.
- With a sharp knife, cut out the pattern you've chosen – work from the outside in, so that you have the messy ends of the cut inside the hollowed-out pumpkin, out of sight.
- Use a tealight as your light source – or two or more, if it's a big pumpkin – as this is probably the most stable. If you really do want to use a candle, make sure there's something in there to hold it up securely.

bonfire night

Bonfire Night shouldn't just be about nipping down to the local firework display. There's something glorious about eating outside in the dark with your hands wrapped around a comforting bowl of stew or soup, and Bonfire Night is the perfect night to do it.

When to have it: This is a night that the kids won't want to miss. Make it a Saturday, and begin just as it starts getting dark – that way you won't freeze to death and everyone can enjoy themselves before bedtime.

What to eat: Warming, wholesome food is the order of the day, whether you dine inside or out. Choose dishes which you can make well in advance, then stick in the oven and reheat if necessary (and of course pick ones which the kids will love).

If you're really brave, you could go the whole hog and light the barbeque – after all it will give everyone something to crowd round and keep warm. This is only advisable if your barbeque has a lid – put it down at regular intervals, otherwise before you know it everyone will be choking to death as the November wind blows smoke into their faces.

Another Bonfire Night staple is hearty baked potatoes. Give them a helping hand with a few minutes in the oven or a quick burst in the microwave, then wrap them in foil and shove them in the embers of the fire, if you're having one. For pud why not roast bananas or pineapple, wrapped in foil, in the fire too? The kids will love toasting marshmallows, but make sure they don't get too close to the fire.

Retreating inside: At some point you'll be beaten inside by the cold weather, especially if it starts to rain. If you are having a lot of guests round you should plan for this by clearing a decent space in the house.

Care for your carpets: On nights like this there's always a lot of tramping in and out of the house, and with it the potential for lots of muddy footprints. Clear out your carpets and strip back to bare floorboards. If you can't then cover them, as your guests won't want to be taking their shoes on and off all the time.

Dress for the worst weather: You'd think it would be obvious that at a bonfire party everyone would dress accordingly, anticipating being outside for part of the night, but what might be obvious to you isn't always obvious to your guests, and there's a good chance that someone will turn up in a dress and coat that are perfect for the local bar, but not for a fireworks party. Plan ahead and dig out a few warm woollies, hats, even coats, and keep them to hand. If you do this in advance, it will save you from hunting them down on the night … with sod's law dictating that you'll have your head in the cupboard while your partner is setting off the fireworks.

Drinks: Wine is probably off the menu, unless it's mulled. Opt instead for hearty, warming, spicy drinks: think cocktails with a kick or a glass of punch to warm the cockles. And again, don't forget the kids: you'll need something for them too, like warm, but not too hot, Ribena.

The fireworks display: If you have a garden and you're brave enough, go for it but take the right precautions. Buy only properly registered fireworks, cordon off a spot in the garden and ensure no one can enter it, even when the fireworks aren't lit.

Once the fireworks start, wheel out that portable stereo and stick on some appropriate music to add an extra atmospheric touch. Then when you've finished the display (or more likely when the rain and/or cold drive you indoors) make sure you keep the party going with a suitable selection of tunes.

Don't forget the sparklers. Buy more than you need, because everyone loves them. Have lots of matches and lighters on hand to light them, and encourage everyone to light up at the same time to enhance the effect.

If you're going to have a bonfire, check first with local authorities to make sure it's safe to burn one. Also, keep a couple of buckets of water and/or a hose to hand.

canapés, amuse-bouches & starters

Dan Redfern

hot-smoked salmon blinis

butter, for frying
25 ready-made cocktail blinis
150ml soured cream
200g hot-smoked salmon (preferably
    kiln-roasted), broken into small pieces
25 capers or caper berries

SERVES FIVE

Hot-smoked salmon is one of my absolute favourite foods and works really well with the blinis. I use salmon that's kiln-roasted and smoked at the same time – it has a lovely honey flavour. I buy it as fillets with the skin on and flake it off into chunks to go on the blinis.

1 Melt a knob of butter in a non-stick frying pan until foaming. Place a batch of blinis in the pan, leaving space between each one. Cook on medium heat for a minute or two on each side until lightly browned, then remove from the pan and drain on kitchen paper.

2 Repeat with more butter and the remaining blinis, taking care that the pan does not get too hot or the butter will burn. If it gets too brown, wipe the pan clean with kitchen paper and start again with fresh butter.

3 Spoon the soured cream on the blinis, then top each one with a piece of salmon and a caper.

Bindi Holding

onion bhajis with spiced yoghurt, coconut & mango sauce

mild olive oil
5 small onions, cut into half-moon slices
¼ tsp chilli powder
½ tsp turmeric
¼ tsp ground ginger
1 tsp ground coriander
½ tsp ground cumin
5 tbsp buckwheat flour
½ tsp salt
1 heaped tsp tomato purée
1¼ shot glasses water
    (or a small egg cup can be used)

FOR THE SAUCE
200ml plain yoghurt
flesh of ½ fresh coconut, grated
flesh of 1 unripe mango, grated
juice of 1–2 lemons
1–2 tsp caster sugar
¼ tsp salt
1 tbsp mild olive oil
2 tsp coriander seeds
1 tsp cumin seeds
1 green chilli, finely chopped (with or
    without seeds according to taste)
8–10 fresh curry or coriander leaves,
    roughly chopped

SERVES FIVE TO SIX

Indian snack food may be a leading cause of our national obesity crisis, but it is delicious. I've taken it out of its oily bath and made it a little less devilish by baking it. It's still tasty, crunchy, moreish and wholly satisfying.

1 Make the sauce. Mix the yoghurt and coconut in a bowl. Add the mango and the juice of 1 lemon with 1 tsp sugar and the salt. Taste and add more lemon juice or sugar if needed.

2 Heat the oil in a frying pan, add the coriander and cumin seeds and fry on low to medium heat until they pop. Add the chilli and curry leaves and cook for 1 minute, then add to the yoghurt. Cover and chill in the fridge for at least 4 hours (or overnight).

3 Make the bhajis: heat a little oil in a large wok or deep frying pan until hot and gently cook the onions until they turn soft and translucent, about 5 minutes. Do not brown or overcook them. Sprinkle in the chilli powder, turmeric and ginger with ½ tsp coriander and ¼ tsp cumin. Stir well and turn off the heat.

4 Preheat the oven to 180°C/Gas 4.

5 Put the buckwheat flour into a bowl. Add the salt and the remaining coriander and cumin and mix well. Now add the onions to the bowl and mix well again until the flour mixture coats the onions.

6 Put the tomato purée into a shot glass or small egg cup and fill with cold water. Mix the purée and water together and pour into the onion mixture. Now fill the shot glass or egg cup just one-quarter full with water, add to the onion mixture and stir well again. Make the mixture wet and easy to stir, but not watery or sloppy. If you have added too much water, add a few pinches of flour until you get the right consistency. If the mixture is a little too thick and dry, add a drop of water at a time until it loosens up.

7 Drizzle a little oil over a large baking tray. Place 2 tbsp of the onion mixture on the tray and flatten a little with the back of a spoon. Repeat to get 5–6 bhajis in total, then drizzle with a little oil. Bake the bhajis for 10 minutes, drizzle a little more oil over them, then bake for a further 5–10 minutes or until they are golden. Serve hot, with the sauce.

Khakan Qureshi

pakoras with yoghurt dip & tomato salad

150g gram flour
about 200ml cold water
1 onion, very finely chopped
6 spring onions, finely chopped
3 green chillies, finely chopped (with
    or without seeds according to taste)
handful of fresh coriander leaves,
    finely chopped
1 tsp salt
1 tsp Madras curry powder (hot or mild)
½ tsp ground coriander
¼ tsp chilli powder (medium, hot or extra
    hot as you like)
1 tsp pomegranate seeds
vegetable oil, for deep-frying

FOR THE DIP
250g plain yoghurt
1 tsp cumin seeds (black ones if available)
2–3 tsp mint sauce (from a jar)
chopped fresh mint or coriander leaves,
    to garnish

FOR THE SALAD
1 onion, finely chopped
½ tsp salt
juice of 1 lemon
2 ripe tomatoes, chopped
1 tsp mint sauce (from a jar)

SERVES SIX

I served pakoras as my starter since they are light, spicy and a fantastic introduction to Indian cuisine. It obviously worked as it prompted my guests to ask for more! They are a perfect accompaniment to any Indian meal.

1 For the dip, mix the yoghurt in a bowl with the cumin seeds. Stir in mint sauce to taste and a pinch each of salt and pepper, then sprinkle the top with chopped mint or coriander. Cover and keep in the fridge until ready to serve.

2 For the salad, put the onion into a bowl and sprinkle with the salt. Leave to soak for 10 minutes. Rinse in a sieve, pat dry with kitchen paper, then tip into a bowl and add the lemon juice. Leave to soak for another 5 minutes. Now mix in the tomatoes, add the mint sauce and stir to coat. Cover and leave at room temperature until serving time.

3 To make the pakoras, put the gram flour into a bowl and gradually mix in the water to make a batter. The consistency should be neither too thick nor too thin, but smooth and creamy enough to pour off a spoon. Now mix in the onion, spring onions, chillies, fresh coriander, salt, spices and pomegranate seeds.

4 Heat the oil in a wok or deep-fat fryer to 180–190°C, or until a teaspoon of the batter rises immediately to the surface when dropped into the hot oil.

5 Take a tablespoon of the batter and lower it carefully into the hot oil. Wait for it to form a small ball or scallop shape before moving on to the next pakora. It's always best to try one as a test first, and then you will get the idea. Some pakoras can become too wet or overcooked – try not to burn!

6 Cook the pakoras for 4–5 minutes, in batches of 4–5 at a time, until golden brown. Remove with a slotted spoon and place on kitchen paper to drain. You will get 12–14 pakoras in total. Serve hot, with the dip and salad.

Paul Condliffe

creamy mushroom bruschetta

30g butter
good-quality olive oil
4 shallots, finely chopped
250g mushrooms, sliced
2 cloves garlic, crushed
150ml double cream
4 thin slices crusty, country-style
    Italian bread
flat-leaf parsley sprigs, to garnish

For this recipe it's all about the quality, the freshness and the types of mushroom you use. Get a mixture – more fungus makes for more fun. Serve on thin slices of bread from a crusty loaf: the crisp crunch of the toast alongside the soft squidge of the mushrooms will create a contrast in textures that's sure to rock your socks off!

1 Heat the butter and a splash of olive oil in a large frying pan until the butter is foaming, and sauté the shallots and mushrooms on medium heat until tender, 5–7 minutes.

2 Add the garlic, then the cream, and salt and pepper to taste. Bring to the boil, stirring, then simmer until the cream has reduced and thickened slightly.

3 Meanwhile, fry the slices of bread in hot olive oil until golden and slightly crisp.

4 Lavish the mushroom mixture on the bread and garnish with parsley. Serve straightaway.

Bindi Holding

romano peppers stuffed with aubergine

1 large aubergine
olive oil
2 Romano peppers
½ tsp cumin seeds
2 cloves garlic, finely chopped
1 chilli (medium or hot, whichever takes
    your fancy), chopped with or without
    the seeds according to taste
large handful of fresh coriander leaves,
    chopped

If you've ever tried feeding your kids aubergine, you may understand the necessity that led to creating this dish. It may be a little devious, but naughty usually leads to tasty and you can't get tastier than this! Coal-grilled aubergine is a flavour to die for, but in the absence of the weather necessary for alfresco cookery you can recreate the flavour with chargrilled Romano peppers. The flavour will come from the seeds, so be sure to cook them well. Serve the pepper halved with the aubergine inside, and your guests won't be able to naysay this fine dish.

1 Preheat the grill on medium-high setting, and line your grill pan with foil.

2 Pierce the aubergine all over with a fork and brush with olive oil. Place in the grill pan and grill for 30 minutes or until soft, turning frequently.

3 While the aubergine is grilling, heat a griddle pan until hot. Halve the peppers lengthways, scoop out and separate the seeds, then brush the peppers with a little olive oil. Now put the peppers skin-side down in the pan, add the seeds and sprinkle with sea salt. Cook on medium heat for about 10 minutes until the pepper skins start to brown, without letting them soften too much and lose their shape. Turn the peppers over and stir the seeds occasionally during this time.

4 When the aubergine is cooked to a soft consistency, remove from the grill and leave until cool enough to handle (about 15 minutes). Now halve the aubergine and scoop out the flesh and any juice into a bowl. Mash the flesh a little with a fork and stir in the fried pepper seeds.

5 Heat a splash of olive oil in a non-stick frying pan until hot and fry the cumin seeds on low to medium heat for a few minutes until they pop and brown. Add the garlic and chilli and cook for a couple more minutes, then add the aubergine to the pan and mix well. Remove from the heat, stir in the coriander and season with salt and pepper to taste.

6 Fill the pepper halves with the aubergine mixture and serve straightaway.

Hayley Williams

caponata on ciabatta

6 large ripe tomatoes
4 tbsp olive oil
1 large onion, chopped
1 aubergine, chopped
1 red pepper, cored, deseeded and chopped
3 sticks celery, chopped
3 cloves garlic, crushed
2 tbsp caster sugar
2 tbsp balsamic vinegar, or more to taste
150g green olives, pitted
1–2 tbsp capers, to taste

TO SERVE
fresh basil leaves
40g pine nuts, toasted
4 slices ciabatta bread, toasted

SERVES FOUR

This versatile dish gets the same reaction every time I make it: 'It's not that pretty but it tastes sensational.' It has been used at both summer barbeques and fancy dinner parties. It really does need to be served at room temperature to let the flavours jump out, with warm, crusty bread on the side. The more balsamic vinegar you add, the bigger the kick!

1 Score a cross in the bottom of each tomato. Put the tomatoes into a large heatproof bowl and cover with boiling water. Leave for about 30 seconds, just until the skins start to peel back, then lift the tomatoes out with a slotted spoon and plunge into a bowl of cold water. Drain, then peel off the skins with your fingers. Chop the flesh into chunks.

2 Heat the olive oil in a large pan. Add the onion, aubergine, red pepper, celery and salt and pepper to taste and fry on high heat for 6 minutes, stirring frequently.

3 Add the tomatoes to the pan with the garlic, sugar, vinegar, olives and capers to taste. Stir and cook on high heat for about 8 minutes or until the aubergine is soft. Taste for seasoning and add more balsamic vinegar if you like.

4 To serve, spoon the caponata into 4 dishes and scatter with basil leaves and toasted pine nuts. Serve at room temperature, with the toasted ciabatta.

David Bell

moules marinières à la crème

1.5kg mussels
15g butter
1 clove garlic, finely chopped
2 shallots, finely chopped
1 bouquet garni (parsley, thyme and
    bay leaves)
100ml dry white wine
125ml double cream
handful of fresh flat-leaf parsley,
    leaves coarsely chopped
crusty bread, to serve

Now, if you really want to impress with little time and effort then this is a great starter. The ingredients are readily available too. Use a decent bottle of wine, as the sauce is the star of the show, and a nice, crusty bread is essential to mop up the best bits. A classic, delicious starter with a minimal amount of fuss – enjoy!

1 Clean the mussels: scrape off any barnacles, then scrub the mussels with a stiff brush under cold running water and remove the beards. Discard any mussels that are open, or that do not close when tapped sharply on the work surface.

2 Melt the butter in a saucepan that is large enough to take all the mussels. Add the garlic, shallots and bouquet garni and soften the shallots for a few minutes on low to medium heat.

3 Add the mussels and wine and turn up the heat to high. Cover the pan tightly and steam the mussels open in their own juices for 3–4 minutes, giving the pan a good shake every now and then.

4 Remove the bouquet garni, pour in the cream and add the parsley. Shake the pan vigorously. Remove from heat and divide between 4 warmed large bowls, discarding any mussels that are closed. Serve with lots of crusty bread.

Sonia Scott McKay

butternut squash soup with nutmeg

1 butternut squash (about 1kg), cut into
    wedges and deseeded
olive oil
a few fresh rosemary sprigs
1 onion, roughly chopped
1 carrot, roughly chopped
1.2 litres good vegetable stock, either
    fresh or made with an organic cube
½ tsp freshly grated nutmeg

TO SERVE
extra virgin olive oil
single cream

This is a great, warming soup. Butternut squash is so easy to prepare as all you need to do is cut, deseed and cook (yes, you can leave the skin on!). For this soup the butternut squash is roasted in the oven with fresh rosemary to give more depth of flavour. My tip for making excellent soup is to use the best stock you can, so avoid stock cubes with monosodium glutamate in them as they leave an unpleasant aftertaste. You could serve it with natural yoghurt instead of cream for a healthier option. I hope you enjoy making and eating this soup as much as me and my dinner guests … happy cooking!

1 Preheat the oven to 200°C/Gas 6.

2 Place the squash wedges flesh-side up in a roasting tin. Drizzle with about 2 tbsp olive oil, season with salt and pepper and scatter over the rosemary sprigs. Roast for 35–40 minutes until the flesh of the squash is soft.

3 Remove the squash from the oven and leave until cool enough to handle, then scoop the pulp from the skin and chop roughly.

4 Heat another 2 tbsp olive oil in a large saucepan until hot and fry the onion and carrot on medium heat for 8–10 minutes, stirring frequently. Pour in the stock and add the chopped squash. Bring to the boil, lower the heat and cover the pan. Simmer gently for 20 minutes, stirring occasionally. Remove from the heat and leave to cool a little.

5 Tip the contents of the pan into a blender and whiz to a purée. Add the nutmeg and taste for seasoning. Serve hot, drizzled with olive oil and cream.

Ita Egan

portobello mushrooms with mozzarella & parma ham

4 large Portobello mushrooms, stalks trimmed
4 knobs of butter
olive oil
4 thin slices Parma ham
4 tsp pesto
1 x 125g ball mozzarella cheese, drained and
   cut into 8 slices

TO SERVE
rocket leaves
balsamic dressing

SERVES FOUR

This dish is a wonderful starter and never fails to impress, yet it's so quick and simple (great for romantic dinners!). Portobello mushrooms have the best taste, but you can use ordinary flat mushrooms too. Make sure you bake them first in plenty of butter before adding the other ingredients, so that they cook through perfectly. I used mozzarella but you can use a stronger cheese like Stilton or goat's cheese. Serve on a bed of rocket with oodles of balsamic drizzle as soon as they come out of the oven, and watch them disappear!

1 Preheat the oven to 200°C/Gas 6.

2 Place the mushrooms gill-side up on a baking tray. Put a knob of butter in the centre of each mushroom, drizzle with a little olive oil and bake for 7–10 minutes. Remove the mushrooms from the oven, leaving the oven on, and set them aside until the sizzling stops and they are cool enough to handle.

3 Lay the ham slices flat on a board and place 1 mushroom in the centre of each slice. Put 1 tsp pesto in the centre of each mushroom followed by 2 slices of mozzarella, then wrap the ham around each mushroom to enclose it completely.

4 Place the parcels on the baking tray and bake for 5 minutes. Serve hot on a bed of rocket drizzled with lots of balsamic dressing.

William Henry

caprese on rustic bread

8 slices rustic Italian bread, such as ciabatta
6–8 ripe plum tomatoes, diced
extra virgin olive oil, for drizzling
1 x 125g ball mozzarella cheese, drained
    and torn into small pieces
handful of fresh basil leaves, torn

I wanted my guests to feel that this was a true Italian evening, so I mirrored the colours of the Italian flag with white mozzarella cheese, green basil leaves and red tomato … *bellissimo*!

1 Toast the bread slices on both sides on a hot griddle pan.

2 Pile the tomatoes on the bread, season with salt and pepper and drizzle with olive oil. Top with the torn mozzarella and basil – and serve straightaway.

Amanda Challener

goat's cheese & red onion tartlets with tomato chutney

FOR THE CHUTNEY
2 large onions, chopped
1 x 400g can chopped tomatoes
85g soft brown sugar
50ml red wine vinegar
1 tbsp balsamic vinegar

FOR THE PASTRY
225g plain flour
pinch of salt
125g butter, cut into small cubes,
    plus extra for greasing
1 medium egg yolk
1–2 tbsp cold water

FOR THE FILLING
25g butter
1 tbsp olive oil
2 large red onions, thinly sliced into
    half-moon shapes
1 tsp soft brown sugar
splash of balsamic vinegar
2 tsp finely chopped fresh sage or thyme,
    plus whole leaves to garnish
100g small goat's cheese cubes,
    roughly broken

SERVES SIX

If you're anything like me, the simpler the recipe the better! Have a go at making these yummy tartlets — they will go down a treat at any dinner party, and are also perfect for a light snack or picnic hamper. And why not be adventurous and vary the fillings to suit the season? Dress them up with a fresh herb salad and a hearty spoonful of delicious homemade chutney on the side.

1 Make the chutney. Put all the ingredients into a pan and bring slowly to the boil on medium heat, stirring occasionally until the sugar has dissolved. Lower the heat and simmer uncovered for 30–35 minutes, stirring regularly, until reduced and thickened. Remove from the heat and leave to cool.

2 Make the pastry. Sift the flour and salt into a large bowl. Drop in the cubes of butter and rub them into the flour until the mixture looks like breadcrumbs. Add the egg yolk and stir it in with enough cold water to make a firm dough. Wrap the dough in clingfilm and chill in the fridge for about 15 minutes.

3 Preheat the oven to 190°C/Gas 5. Butter 6 x 9cm loose-bottomed tartlet tins.

4 Remove the clingfilm and roll the dough out on a lightly floured surface until about 2mm thick. Cut 6 x 11cm discs out of the pastry, then use to line the tartlet tins. Prick the pastry on the bottom with a fork and line the tarts with greaseproof paper or foil and fill with baking beans. Bake blind for 15 minutes, then remove the paper and beans and bake for a further 5–8 minutes until the pastry is cooked.

5 Make the filling while the pastry is baking. Heat the butter and oil in a deep frying pan until the butter is foaming, add the onions and sugar and cook on low to medium heat for about 15 minutes until golden and caramelized. Now add a splash of balsamic vinegar and the chopped sage or thyme, and season to taste.

6 Divide the onions between the tart cases and top with the goat's cheese. Return to the oven for 7–10 minutes before serving, just until the cheese starts to melt and brown.

7 Remove the tartlets from the tins, place on plates and garnish with sage or thyme leaves. Serve the tarts warm, with the chutney.

Annette Evans

aubergine & manchego tarts with slow-roasted tomatoes

FOR THE PASTRY
250g plain flour
125g butter, melted
125g Parmesan cheese, grated
pinch of cayenne pepper
3–4 tbsp cold water

FOR THE TOPPING
350g cherry tomatoes
2 large cloves garlic, sliced
8 tbsp olive oil
1 large aubergine
handful of fresh basil leaves, chopped,
      plus 8 small basil sprigs
150g Manchego cheese, shaved

SERVES EIGHT

I love aubergine and feel that it is an underrated but incredibly versatile vegetable. It's great in stews or lasagnes, but here I wanted an unusual combination of flavours and textures that looked great too. You can make the pastry a few days in advance and store it in an airtight tin. This was a hit starter, not just for *Come Dine With Me* but for my friends as well. You could also make the portions smaller and substitute sun-blushed tomatoes for roasted tomatoes and use as canapés.

1 Preheat the oven to 190°C/Gas 5.

2 Make the pastry. Put all the ingredients into a food processor with 3 tbsp cold water and mix to form a dough, adding a little more water if necessary. Turn out on to a lightly floured surface, roll to a thickness of about 5mm, and cut into 8 rectangles, each about 10 x 7cm. Place the rectangles on a baking sheet and bake for 15 minutes.

3 Remove the rectangles from the oven and keep warm. Lower the oven temperature to 150°C/Gas 2.

4 Put the tomatoes and garlic for the topping on a baking tray, sprinkle with 3 tbsp of the olive oil and slow-roast for 45 minutes.

5 Meanwhile, cut the aubergine on the diagonal into 8 slices, each about 1cm thick. Place the slices in a shallow dish, season well with salt and pepper and add the remaining olive oil and the chopped basil. Toss the aubergine slices so that they become coated in oil on both sides. Cover and leave to marinate for 20 minutes.

6 Heat a griddle pan until hot and fry the aubergine slices for 8–10 minutes, turning occasionally, until softened and juicy. Remove from the pan and drain on kitchen paper.

7 Assemble the tarts: place 1 pastry rectangle on each plate, and add some Manchego shavings, a slice of aubergine, 3–4 roasted tomatoes and some garlic slices. Drizzle with the juice from the tomatoes and garnish with the basil sprigs.

main courses

Milly Johnson

chicken fricassée

25g butter
225g mushrooms (assorted or button), roughly sliced
50g butter
50g plain flour
400ml milk
1 chicken stock cube
150ml dry white wine
50g Gruyère cheese, grated
4 ready-roasted chicken breasts, skinned and chopped into chunks

SERVES FOUR

This has been a signature dish of mine for as long as I can remember, because it's so adaptable. The Gruyère gives it a fabulous full flavour which goes beautifully with vegetables, rice or pasta, as well as making a perfect pie filling! It's also nice with big chunks of ham or sweetcorn in it, for further variations. Since this dish is very rich, plain vegetable accompaniments are best, such as asparagus batons, baby carrots, baby sweetcorn, rice or potatoes boulangère.

1 Melt 25g butter in a frying pan on medium heat until foaming. Add the mushrooms and fry for about 10 minutes until they are tender and the liquid has gone, stirring frequently. Remove from the heat and set aside.

2 Make a white sauce: melt 50g butter in a large saucepan on medium heat, add the flour and cook on low heat, stirring, for a couple of minutes. Remove from the heat and slowly add the milk, whisking well after each addition. Put the sauce back on the heat and bring to a simmer, whisking constantly to prevent lumps forming.

3 Crumble the stock cube into the sauce, pour in the wine and bring back to a simmer, whisking vigorously. Now add the Gruyère and cook on low heat, stirring all the time, until the cheese melts and you have a smooth sauce.

4 Add the mushrooms and chicken to the sauce and stir until evenly combined. Taste and season with salt and pepper before serving.

Vanessa Boukharouba

duck with olives & pomme purée

1 x 2.5kg duck, cut into quarters
225g small shallots, peeled
½ tsp caster sugar
2 tbsp plain flour
250ml red wine
250ml chicken stock
1 bouquet garni
115g pitted olives (green or black)

FOR THE POMME PURÉE
900g floury potatoes (such as Maris Piper
    or King Edward), cut into large chunks
75–100g Comté cheese, grated

FOR THE CARROTS
500g Chantenay carrots
generous knob of butter
1 tsp caster sugar
1 tsp salt
snipped chives, to garnish

SERVES FOUR

Sophisticated slow-cooked recipes are hard to come by, but this one is just that! With the preparation done in advance, this will leave you plenty of time to enjoy the party.

1 Preheat the oven to 200°C/Gas 6.

2 Heat a large frying pan on medium heat until hot. Place the duck pieces skin-side down in the pan and cook for about 10 minutes to brown the skin. Transfer the pieces to a large casserole, placing them skin-side up.

3 Drain all but 1 tbsp of the duck fat from the frying pan. Place the pan on high heat, add the shallots and cook for a few minutes until they begin to colour. Lower the heat to medium, sprinkle over the sugar and cook for 5 minutes or until the shallots are golden. Sprinkle in the flour and cook for 2 minutes, stirring constantly, then gradually pour in the wine and stock, stirring well. Season to taste and bring to the boil, pour over the duck and add the bouquet garni and salt and pepper to taste. Cover the casserole and cook in the oven for 1 hour.

4 Turn the heat down to 160°C/Gas 3 and cook the duck for a further 2 hours.

5 For the pomme purée, put the potatoes into a large saucepan of cold salted water, cover and bring to the boil on high heat. Lower the heat to medium and simmer for 15–20 minutes until the potatoes are tender. Drain the potatoes and return to the pan to dry out on low heat for a minute or two, then mash to a lump-free purée. Stir the cheese into the purée and spoon into an ovenproof dish. Put in the oven with the duck for the final 30 minutes to heat through and brown.

6 Put the olives into a bowl and cover with boiling water. Leave to stand for about 2 minutes, then drain and add to the duck for the final 20 minutes.

7 Meanwhile, put the whole carrots into a saucepan with the butter, sugar and salt. Cover generously with water and bring to the boil, then boil until the carrots are tender and the liquid is reduced and syrupy, about 15 minutes. Remove from the heat and sprinkle with black pepper and chives.

8 Skim the fat off the duck before serving with the pomme purée and carrots.

Gill Buley

boeuf stroganoff

800g rib-eye steak, cut into thin strips
2 tbsp olive oil
1 tbsp balsamic vinegar
1 tsp paprika
2 tbsp brandy
1 large onion, finely chopped
300g small button mushrooms, either
    whole or halved
250ml crème fraîche or double cream

TO SERVE
truffle oil (optional)
chopped fresh flat-leaf parsley
boiled rice

Boeuf stroganoff is a favourite of mine, a special treat that I order whenever I see it on the menu when holidaying in the Mediterranean. I love the whole performance, when the waiter flambés it at your table. The problem is replicating it back home, since it's hard to get it right. Even if I use the best fillet steak it never tastes quite as tender, so I experimented with other cuts of beef and found that this dish works well with rib-eye. In my experience, if you ever want to spoil the man in your life then you're on to a winner.

1 Put the strips of steak into a large bowl with 1 tbsp of the olive oil and the balsamic vinegar. Add the paprika and pepper to taste and stir well to mix. Cover and leave to marinate for an hour or so.

2 Heat a large, deep sauté pan or flameproof casserole until hot. Place about a third of the steak in the pan and sauté on medium heat until browned on all sides – about 5 minutes. Repeat with the remaining steak, then return all of the meat to the pan and remove from the heat.

3 Heat the brandy very gently in a small saucepan, just until warmed through. Remove from the heat, pour the warm brandy over the steak and ignite with a long taper or match. Wait until the flames have died down completely, then remove the steak from the pan and let it rest while you prepare the sauce.

4 Heat the remaining oil in the pan and fry the onion over low heat for 5 minutes. Add the mushrooms and cook for 10 minutes on medium heat until the onions are glossy, the mushrooms are cooked and all the juices have gone.

5 Add the crème fraîche and salt and pepper to taste, stir well and bring to a simmer. Return the steak to the pan and warm through, stirring constantly.

6 Spoon the stroganoff on to 4 warmed plates, drizzle with truffle oil if you like, and sprinkle with parsley. Serve straightaway, with boiled rice.

Adam Baker

duck breasts with port, black cherry & pomegranate jus

7.5cm piece fresh root ginger
4 x 175g duck breasts, trimmed of excess fat

FOR THE JUS
300ml port
300ml chicken stock
2 tsp pomegranate molasses, or more to taste
10 dried black cherries, soaked in hot water
    for 30 minutes and drained

FOR THE PURÉE
30g butter
2 tbsp olive oil
1 onion, chopped
2 cloves garlic, chopped
2 x 400g cans butter beans, drained and rinsed
4 tbsp dry white wine
about 125ml chicken stock

Don't go quackers over cooking duck! The trick is to score the skin and to heat the pan slowly. This process allows the fat to escape, making the duck even more tasty and the skin nice and crispy!

1 Grate the ginger into a dish large enough to hold the duck breasts in a single layer, then press with the back of a metal spoon to squeeze out the juice; discard the grated ginger. Lay the duck breasts flesh-side down in the juice, cover and marinate for 1 hour.

2 Make the purée. Heat half the butter with the oil in a saucepan on medium heat until foaming. Add the onion and garlic and sauté until soft, 5–8 minutes. Add the beans and remaining butter, the wine and 125ml stock. Bring to the boil, stirring, then simmer for 5 minutes. Leave to cool slightly before whizzing to a smooth purée in a blender, adding more stock if too thick. Season, transfer to a clean pan and set aside.

3 Preheat the oven to 200°C/Gas 6.

4 Dry the duck with kitchen paper and score criss-cross lines in the skin to make small diamond shapes. Rub the skin with a little salt and pepper. Place the duck skin-side down in a large non-stick frying pan that will go in the oven. Place the pan on medium heat and heat slowly for about 5 minutes to render the fat. Turn the duck over, increase the heat to high and sear the flesh side for 2 minutes. Transfer the duck breasts to a shallow roasting tray, keeping them skin-side up, and roast for 6–8 minutes.

5 Meanwhile, pour off most of the duck fat from the frying pan and place the pan on medium to high heat. Deglaze the pan with the port, pour in the stock and boil to reduce by half. Keep this jus on a gentle simmer.

6 Remove the duck from the oven, place in a shallow dish and leave in a warm place for 10 minutes. Pour the juices from the tray into the simmering jus, stir in the molasses and cherries and simmer for 5 minutes. Taste the jus for seasoning and add more molasses if you like, then simmer until reduced to your liking.

7 To serve, reheat the bean purée, adding a little stock or water if necessary. Slice the duck and arrange on 4 warmed plates. Spoon the jus over and serve with the bean purée.

Gary Holden

rossini-style tournedos with porcini & red wine sauce

5 tournedos steaks, cut 2.5cm thick and tied
with string
4 tbsp olive oil
5 large flat mushrooms (Portobello are good),
stalk ends trimmed
125g smooth liver pâté, softened

FOR THE SAUCE
10g dried porcini
150ml hot water
4 shallots, finely chopped with skins left on
1 clove garlic, finely chopped with skin left on
125ml red wine
300ml good beef stock
2 tsp Henderson's relish (or Worcestershire
sauce or balsamic vinegar), or more to taste
25g butter, cut into small cubes

This combination evolved from a birthday meal that was cooked for me by my wife on the day that I found out I was to appear on the show. The porcini add a real earthy depth of flavour, and the pâté adds a rich velvety surprise!

1 Season the steaks with freshly ground black pepper and brush with 1 tbsp olive oil. Cover and set aside.

2 Put the porcini for the sauce into a bowl, pour in the hot water and leave to soak for about 30 minutes. Drain, reserving the liquid, then dry the porcini on kitchen paper and chop finely.

3 Continue with the sauce. Heat a frying pan on medium heat until hot. Put the shallots and garlic in the pan and dry-fry for about 10 minutes until very brown, stirring frequently. Deglaze the pan with the wine, increase the heat to high and add the stock with the reserved porcini liquid and 2 tsp relish. Boil, stirring, for 5 minutes or until reduced – the liquid should generously cover the shallots. Now pass the sauce through a sieve, pressing hard on the shallots to extract as much juice as possible. Return the sieved sauce to the pan and add the porcini, then taste for seasoning and add more relish if you like. Set aside.

4 Preheat the oven to 150°C/Gas 2.

5 Heat the remaining 3 tbsp olive oil in a large frying pan until hot. Place the flat mushrooms in the pan and fry on low to medium heat for 6–8 minutes or until tender, flipping them over when necessary. Transfer the mushrooms gill-side up to a baking dish and divide the pâté between them, smoothing it out evenly. Cover the dish with foil and keep warm in the oven.

6 Season the steaks with salt. Heat a griddle pan on high heat until very hot. Place the steaks on the pan, turn the heat down to medium and cook the steaks to your liking: 2–4 minutes on each side for rare to medium-rare meat. Remove the steaks from the pan and leave to rest in a warm place for 5 minutes. Meanwhile, reheat the sauce and whisk in the butter.

7 Remove the string from the steaks. Place the steaks on the pâté-filled mushrooms on 5 warmed plates (or place the mushrooms on the steaks if you prefer) and drizzle with the sauce. Serve straightaway.

Harry Ioannou

sea bass with roasted vegetables & pourgouri pilaf

4 whole sea bass (about 500g each), gutted and left whole with heads and tails on
olive oil
8 sprigs fresh rosemary
2 cloves garlic, thinly sliced
Greek yoghurt, to serve

FOR THE VEGETABLES
olive oil
1 courgette, sliced
1 red pepper, cored, deseeded and sliced
1 yellow pepper, cored, deseeded and sliced
1 aubergine, sliced
1 small fennel bulb, sliced
6 small onions, peeled
4 cloves garlic, peeled
1 tsp dried basil
1 tsp ground cumin
1 tsp ground coriander

FOR THE PILAF
75g pourgouri (bulgur wheat)
300ml cold water
2 tbsp olive oil
50–60g dried vermicelli, broken into small pieces
½ x 400g can chopped tomatoes

SERVES FOUR

I chose this dish as it is very simple to prepare. The Greeks are by nature a very gregarious race and would rather spend time round the table with their guests than in the kitchen preparing a fancy meal that will get eaten in 5 minutes. That is why if you look at any Greek menu it contains simple food prepared with fresh, locally sourced ingredients, and is generally very healthy.

1 Preheat the oven to 190°C/Gas 5. Brush 2 large earthenware baking dishes with olive oil.

2 Place the sliced vegetables in one of the dishes with the whole onions and garlic, the basil and spices and salt and pepper to taste. Add a good splash of olive oil and toss everything together until well mixed. Place in the oven and roast for 1 hour.

3 Meanwhile, open out the fish to expose the white flesh. Rub olive oil liberally over the flesh and sprinkle with salt. Place 2 rosemary sprigs and a few slices of garlic inside each fish, then close the fish up and rub olive oil and salt into the skin.

4 Arrange the fish in a single layer in the second earthenware dish, place in the oven and roast for 15–20 minutes. The fish is done when the flesh flakes easily with a fork and is still very moist – do not overcook or the fish will be dry.

5 While the vegetables and fish are roasting, make the pilaf. Put the bulgur wheat and water into a saucepan and bring to the boil on high heat. Lower the heat to a simmer and cook for about 10 minutes, stirring frequently, until all the water is absorbed and the wheat is soft.

6 Meanwhile, heat the olive oil in a non-stick frying pan until hot and stir-fry the vermicelli on low to medium heat for a few minutes until they turn golden brown. Add the tomatoes and stir briskly to mix, then simmer for a couple of minutes.

7 Add the vermicelli mixture to the wheat and toss to combine. Taste for seasoning and stir in ½ cup of water if it seems a little dry.

8 Serve each person with a whole fish and a portion of vegetables and pilaf. Hand yoghurt round separately in a bowl.

Jodie Marsh

twice-baked cheese soufflés on portobello mushrooms with ratatouille

FOR THE SOUFFLÉ
softened butter, for greasing
300g light soft cheese
4 large eggs, separated
150g extra-strong mature Cheddar
    cheese, grated
150ml double cream
50g Parmesan cheese, freshly grated

FOR THE RATATOUILLE
1 red onion, chopped
5 cloves garlic, crushed
50g butter
2 tbsp olive oil
1 aubergine, chopped
2 courgettes, chopped
1 green pepper, cored, deseeded and chopped
1 tbsp red wine vinegar
1 tbsp tomato purée
2 bay leaves
¼ tsp cayenne pepper
5 vine-ripened tomatoes, roughly chopped

FOR THE MUSHROOMS
3–4 tbsp olive oil
25g butter
4 large Portobello mushrooms, stalk ends
    trimmed

SERVES FOUR

These babies won me the show! The beauty of the twice-baked method is that you can prepare them earlier and then re-bake them exactly when you need to.

1 Preheat the oven to 200°C/Gas 6. Grease 4 x 200ml soufflé dishes or ramekins with lots of butter and stand the dishes in a roasting tin.

2 Make the soufflé mix. Put the soft cheese into a large bowl, add the egg yolks and beat well until soft and creamy. Add the Cheddar cheese and season to taste. In a separate large bowl and using electric beaters, whisk the egg whites to stiff peaks. Gently fold the egg whites into the cheese mixture until evenly incorporated.

3 Spoon the mixture into the soufflé dishes, then run the tip of a sharp knife around the edge of each soufflé to release it from the side of the dish. Pour cold water into the roasting tin to come halfway up the sides of the dishes. Bake for 20 minutes or until the soufflés are well risen and golden on top, with a slight wobble in the centre when shaken. Leave to cool (if not serving the same day, cover with clingfilm and keep in the fridge).

4 Make the ratatouille. In a large saucepan, soften the onion and garlic in the butter and oil for 5–8 minutes. Add the remaining ingredients, season to taste and stir well. Cover and cook on low heat for 30 minutes, stirring often. Remove the bay leaves and set aside (if not serving the same day, keep in the fridge).

5 When you are ready to serve, preheat the oven to 200°C/Gas 6. If the soufflés have been in the fridge, remove them for 10–15 minutes before baking, to take the chill off.

6 Cook the mushrooms. Heat the oil and butter in a frying pan until the butter is foaming. Place the mushrooms in the pan and fry on low to medium heat for 6–8 minutes or until tender, flipping them over when necessary.

7 Place the mushrooms gill-side up on a baking tray. Turn each soufflé out of its dish and place the right way up in each of the mushrooms. Pour the cream over the top and sprinkle with the grated Parmesan. Bake for 15 minutes or until risen again. At the same time, reheat the ratatouille until bubbling, adding a splash or two of hot water if necessary. Taste for seasoning before serving with the soufflés.

desserts

Coranne Denham

tipsy chocolate mousse

350g chocolate chips
2 tbsp dark rum, or a little flick of
    the wrist more
1 tbsp espresso coffee (or use instant –
    1 tsp dissolved in 2 tbsp hot water)
500ml whipping cream

SERVES FOUR

This was given to me by my friend Rosie and is the easiest chocolate mousse ever. It keeps for a few days in the fridge, and is so moreish you will keep going back to the fridge for a spoonful. Different alcohol can be substituted, but it works best with dark rum, and best of all with Bermuda dark rum. It's so easy it can be made in 10 minutes.

1 Put the chocolate chips, rum and coffee into a heatproof bowl set over a pan of gently simmering water and heat together until melted and smooth, stirring occasionally. Remove the bowl from the pan and leave the chocolate to cool to room temperature.

2 Whip the cream in a bowl until stiff peaks form.

3 Stir some of the cream into the melted chocolate mixture to loosen it, then fold in the rest until the mixture is smooth and evenly blended. Transfer to a serving bowl, cover and keep in the fridge until ready to serve.

Gary Holden

poached pears with honey & walnut cream

5 large, hard pears (such as Rocha, Conference or Green Williams)
750ml Marsala wine
50g caster sugar
1 cinnamon stick
1 vanilla pod, split lengthways
3 tsp arrowroot

FOR THE CREAM
275–300ml double cream
3 tbsp runny honey
40g chopped walnuts

This is an old favourite, and works every time! Be careful not to over-cook the pears as they will become soft and mushy. Instead of the Marsala you can use red wine or cider as the poaching liquid.

1 Carefully peel the pears with a vegetable peeler, maintaining the shape of the fruit. Leave the stalks on, but cut a thin slice from the bottom of each pear to enable it to stand upright.

2 Lay the pears on their sides in a large saucepan or flameproof casserole and pour the Marsala over them. Add the sugar, cinnamon stick and vanilla pod and bring to simmering point on medium heat. Cover the pan and simmer the pears gently for about 30 minutes until tender when pierced with a cocktail stick. Gently shake the pan and turn the pears over occasionally during this time, to make sure they cook and colour evenly.

3 When the pears are cooked, let them cool in the poaching liquid (you can leave them in the fridge overnight), then lift them out with a slotted spoon and set aside. Strain the liquid into a clean pan, place on medium heat and bring to a simmer.

4 Mix the arrowroot with a little water to make a smooth paste. Slowly pour the paste into the simmering liquid, stirring all the time, and boil until the liquid thickens and becomes glossy – you may not need all of the paste. Remove from the heat and cool, then pour over the pears in a serving dish. Cover with clingfilm and chill in the fridge until serving time.

5 To serve, whip the cream in a bowl until soft peaks form. Add the honey and walnuts and fold together. Spoon some sauce on to 5 plates. Stand the pears upright in the sauce, spoon over more sauce and add a generous helping of the cream.

Phil Davies

blackberry & apple pie

FOR THE SHORTCRUST PASTRY
250g plain flour
pinch of salt
1 tsp caster sugar
75g butter, diced
50g lard, diced
50ml cold water
1 medium egg white, lightly broken
    up with a fork

FOR THE FILLING
juice of ½ lemon
550g Bramley cooking apples
65g soft brown sugar
¼ tsp ground nutmeg
2 star anise
150g blackberries
1 tbsp arrowroot or cornflour
2 tbsp stem ginger syrup (from a jar)
pinch of ground cinnamon
2 tsp caster sugar

Nature's really great, the way she throws such fabulous partners together: ripe blackberries in the hedgerows alongside Bramleys on the tree. That couldn't be fresher, couldn't be cheaper! Then just to remind us of the summer we've left behind, this pie is all warmed up with Middle Eastern spices.

1 Make the pastry. Put the flour, salt, sugar and fats into a food processor and pulse to create a breadcrumb texture. Add the water a little at a time until a dough forms. Remove and shape into a ball, wrap in clingfilm and chill in the fridge for about 30 minutes.

2 For the filling, pour the lemon juice into a large bowl of cold water and stir well. Peel, core and slice the apples, putting them into the lemon water as soon as you slice them.

3 Preheat the oven to 190°C/Gas 5.

4 Unwrap the dough and divide in half. Roll out one half very thinly on a lightly floured surface and use to line a 23cm round pie dish that is 4cm deep. Trim the edge and brush the pastry all over with some of the egg white.

5 Drain the sliced apples very well and pat dry with kitchen paper. Mix the brown sugar in a small bowl with the nutmeg and star anise. Now layer the apples in the pie dish with the blackberries, dusting with a little arrowroot or cornflour and the spiced sugar as you go. When you have finished layering, pour the ginger syrup over the top.

6 Roll out the remaining pastry for the pie lid. Brush the exposed pastry lip with egg white and top with the pastry lid. Seal and trim the edge, fluting it in a decorative pattern if you like, and cut 2 small steam vents in the lid.

7 Mix the cinnamon with the caster sugar. Brush the pie with the remaining egg white mixed with a little water, then sprinkle with the cinnamon sugar. Stand the dish on a baking sheet and bake for 35 minutes, then allow to rest for about 30 minutes so the fruit can absorb some of the juices. Serve the pie warm, telling your guests to keep an eye out for the 2 star anise.

Ian Jones

chocolate cheesecake

50g whole unblanched almonds
65g butter, plus extra for greasing
175g digestive biscuits
150g dark chocolate, broken into small pieces
350g full-fat soft cheese, at room temperature
200ml crème fraîche
2 large eggs, separated
50g golden caster sugar
3 tbsp cold water
1½ tsp agar flakes
chocolate curls and cocoa powder, to decorate

I was nervous with this one as I could not use gelatine for religious reasons, so I had to use a setting agent called agar flakes. Use a good-quality dark chocolate as this gives the best flavour. To all you chocoholics . . .

1 Preheat the oven to 200°C/Gas 6. Butter a 20cm springform or loose-bottomed cake tin.

2 Spread the almonds out on a baking tray and roast for 7–8 minutes or until toasted. Cool slightly, then chop finely. Melt the butter in a small pan.

3 Place the biscuits in a plastic bag and crush into fine crumbs with a rolling pin. Transfer to a bowl and add the almonds and melted butter. Stir to mix, then press over the bottom of the cake tin. Chill in the fridge while preparing the filling.

4 For the filling, melt the chocolate in a bowl over a pan of gently simmering water, ensuring the water does not touch the bottom of the bowl. Remove the bowl from the pan and leave the chocolate to cool to room temperature.

5 Beat the cheese in another bowl with the crème fraîche, egg yolks and sugar. Put the 3 tbsp cold water into a small pan, sprinkle over the agar flakes and let them dissolve completely on low heat, stirring occasionally. This should take 5–8 minutes. Stir quickly into the cheese mix followed by the cooled, melted chocolate.

6 Whisk the egg whites to soft peaks in a clean bowl, then very gently fold one-third at a time into the chocolate mixture. Spoon over the biscuit base, level the surface and chill for at least 4 hours or overnight.

7 Remove the cheesecake from the tin and place on a serving plate. Decorate with chocolate curls and a dusting of cocoa powder just before serving.

Nicola T

nikki's naughty chocolate surprise

1 x 230g bar milk chocolate
1 x 600ml carton double cream
2 tbsp icing sugar, sifted
capful of Baileys
100g chocolate digestive biscuits, crushed
knob of butter
1 vanilla pod, split lengthways and seeds
    scraped out
12 giant chocolate buttons, to decorate

I don't really make desserts at home so I had to come
up with something the other WAGs would like. Obviously
all girls like chocolate, so it was always going to include
chocolate! In M&S you get these sundaes in a pot which
I really like, so I tried to make my own version of a dessert
like that and this is what I came up with.

1 Set aside 30g of the chocolate, then break the remainder
into squares. Put half the squares into a heatproof bowl
set over a pan of gently simmering water and heat gently,
stirring occasionally, until the chocolate has melted.
Remove the bowl from the pan and leave the chocolate
to cool to room temperature.

2 Whip half the cream with the sugar until it holds its
shape. Combine with the Baileys and the melted chocolate
to make a mousse. Divide the mousse in half, mix the
crushed biscuits into one half and spoon into 6 x 200ml
glasses or dishes.

3 Melt the remaining chocolate squares the same way
as the first, remove the bowl from the pan and stir in
the butter and 2 tbsp of the remaining cream to stop
the chocolate hardening. Cool slightly, then spoon and
spread over the mousse in the glasses.

4 Spoon the remaining mousse over the chocolate layer.
Whip the remaining cream with the vanilla seeds until
it holds its shape, then swirl on top of the mousse.

5 To serve, grate the reserved chocolate over the cream
and decorate each serving with 2 chocolate buttons.

January Jone-Omotajo

grandma's apple pie

375g shortcrust pastry
knob of butter, melted
vanilla ice cream, to serve

FOR THE FILLING
1kg juicy cooking apples, peeled,
    cored and sliced
100g caster sugar
½ tsp ground cinnamon
¼ tsp ground nutmeg
juice of 1 lemon
1 tsp vanilla extract
3 tbsp plain flour

SERVES SIX

I cannot take any credit for this recipe: it's all grandma. She blesses us with her amazing apple pie at Thanksgiving, Christmas, Easter and any other family holiday or get-together that we have. It is the perfect ending to a family meal – sweet, rich and decadent. Grandma's apple pie tastes delicious with or without ice cream and is even better when warmed. Yummy!

1 Preheat the oven to 190°C/Gas 5.

2 Prepare the filling. Combine the sliced apples in a large bowl with the sugar, cinnamon, nutmeg, lemon juice, vanilla and flour.

3 Roll out the pastry on a lightly floured surface until about 3mm thick and use two-thirds to line a 20cm pie dish, leaving a slight overhang,

4 Pile the apple mixture in the dish. Roll out the remaining pastry to make a lid. Dampen the pastry rim with cold water and lay the lid over the top of the apples. Seal and trim the edges, then make a decorative pattern around the edge with a fork if you like. Make a couple of slits in the lid to allow steam to escape.

5 Brush the pastry with melted butter and bake the pie for 45 minutes. The pie is ready when the top is golden and the apples are tender when pierced through the pastry with a skewer. Serve warm, with vanilla ice cream.

Dane Bowers

chocolate bread & butter pudding with baileys

12 slices day-old white bread from
    a large loaf, cut 1.5cm thick
75g butter, softened
1 x 135g bar Galaxy caramel chocolate,
    broken into squares
3 large eggs
25g caster sugar
350ml milk
300ml Baileys
demerara sugar, for sprinkling

TO SERVE
300ml double cream
4 tbsp Baileys

SERVES SIX TO EIGHT

I think this is what won me the show. It's so easy to make too! Bread and butter pudding has been around for yonks but mine's a bit different – I added chunks of Galaxy caramel chocolate and Baileys to make it taste amazing! I also offered Baileys mixed with some cream to pour over each portion – you can't go wrong with a bit of Baileys!

1 Spread the bread with the butter, cut off and discard the crusts, then cut the bread into triangles. Arrange half the triangles in a buttered 30 x 23cm baking dish, overlapping them slightly and tucking half the squares of chocolate at regular intervals underneath.

2 Whisk the eggs in a bowl with the sugar, milk and Baileys. Pour half this custard mixture over the bread and press the bread down into the liquid. Allow to stand for about 10 minutes for the bread to absorb the liquid.

3 Arrange the remaining bread and chocolate in the dish as before, then pour the remainder of the custard mixture on top. Press the bread well down to submerge it in the liquid, then place in the fridge for about 30 minutes to let the liquid be thoroughly absorbed by the bread.

4 Preheat the oven to 180°C/Gas 4.

5 Sprinkle the pudding with demerara sugar and bake for 30 minutes or until tinged golden brown. Serve hot, with a jug of the cream and Baileys mixed together.

Rob Hubbard

tarte tatin

250g puff pastry
4–5 large dessert apples
75g caster sugar
75g butter, cut into cubes
soured cream or Greek yoghurt, to serve

I often travel to France and love their tartes tatin. Normally you get it served cold or warmed through, but once in a small mountain hut of a restaurant they made it to order. I asked the owner how he did it and he gave me the recipe, which was so simple that I remembered it and tried it when I got home. Here it is!

1 Roll out the pastry on a lightly floured surface until about 1cm thick and 2.5cm larger than the diameter of the pan you are going to use. A non-stick 20cm omelette pan is ideal, but you can use one slightly larger if that is what you've got.

2 Cut the apples into quarters, then peel and core them. If you are using a larger pan, you will probably need 5 apples.

3 Put the sugar and butter into the pan and heat gently on low heat until the sugar has dissolved, shaking the pan occasionally. Increase the heat to medium and cook for about 10 minutes to a light caramel colour. If the sugar crystallizes during this time, stir in a little hot water from the kettle (use a long-handled spoon as the mixture will splutter) and keep stirring vigorously until the caramel is smooth.

4 Arrange the apples in the pan so that they fill the pan snugly and cook for about 20 minutes until they are caramelized and just soft. Remove the pan from the heat and leave to cool for 10–15 minutes.

5 Meanwhile, preheat the oven to 200°C/Gas 6. If the handle of your pan isn't ovenproof, wrap it well with foil.

6 Lay the pastry over the pan and tuck in the overhang, pushing it down between the apples and the inside edge of the pan.

7 Bake for 30 minutes or until the pastry is risen, firm and golden brown. Leave to settle for 5 minutes before turning out upside down on to a serving plate. Serve warm, with soured cream or Greek yoghurt.

winter

With the arrival of winter comes the full harvest of root vegetables, and this new season also rivals autumn as the best time of year to enjoy a great range of meats. All eyes are on turkey in the run-up to Christmas – and of course that also means sprouts. But let's not forget that winter entertaining isn't all about 25 December: there are drinks parties to be had before and after the big day, the New Year to be celebrated, and Valentine's Day for romantic meals for two.

Vegetables

Beetroot
Brussels sprouts (December/January)
Cabbage: red, savoy, white (December)
Carrots
Cauliflower
Celeriac
Kale
Leeks
Parsnips
Potatoes
Purple sprouting broccoli (February)
Shallots (February)
Spinach
Swede (December)

Fruit

Apples
Pears

Meat

Goose
Partridge
Pheasant
Turkey
Wild rabbit

Fish

Carp
John Dory
Lemon sole (February)
Mussels (December)
Oysters
Sea bass
Skate (January/February)
Turbot
Wild salmon (February)

the pre-christmas mulled wine and mince pie party

A mulled wine and mince pie party on a suitable Sunday in December can be a great way of getting into the festive spirit. Here are a few tips on how to make it work.

Mince pies: If it's your first time, make more than you think you need. You don't want them to run out, and if there are some left over then you can give them to your guests to take away (unless they've already eaten six and can no longer stand the sight of them). Alternatively you can always freeze them for Christmas, eat them for the rest of the week, give them to an old people's home or, if you don't care that your work-mates will guess that you've had a party without them, take them to work.

Make sure you use the oven timer if you're planning to heat them up during the party. Four hours in, with the mulled wine taking its toll, it's all too easy to forget about them and remember only when someone asks, 'Do I smell burning?'

Wine: Unlike any other party, for this event you'll be warming the wine in a pan. There are four options:

1 Buy more than enough on sale or return, then you'll only need to mull your own wine and keep topping it up from your supplies. You can then drink the wine which your guests bring another time. Opt for this if you like red wine and, more importantly, if you can trust your mates to bring decent bottles which you're happy to drink your way through.

2 Try to persuade as many of your guests as possible to bring the same red. When you're buying in a quantity of your own wine, choose a bog-standard red which is widely available. Then you can say to those mates who will get the hint/are understanding in the matter, 'If you were thinking of bringing a bottle and enjoy mulled wine, please try to bring [insert bog-standard red here].' When your wine supply dries out you can tuck into everyone else's bottles, but be warned that mulled wine slips down more easily than ordinary plonk and you'll inevitably need more than you expect. This leads us on to the third option …

3 Mull the various wines which people bring in small quantities in different saucepans. Alternatively, take the risky option and chuck it all into the same pan. Be warned, though, that mixing wines is unpredictable and might be frowned on if you have a wine bore at the party.

4 Of course there is an even easier option, which is to buy ready-mulled wine from a supermarket or offie – again try to do a bit of research for sale-or-return purchases. If you can't do that, make sure you have some mulling sachets up your sleeve just in case you run out and need to crack into the red wine supplies brought by your guests. If you're feeling really brave you can mull white wine as well, just in case any of your guests are red-wine-phobes – they'll love your party even more if you've made the effort to cater for them! Drier wines like Rieslings and Viogniers work best.

Other drink: Remember that not everyone likes mulled wine, so get other booze in too, along with a selection of soft drinks.

What time of day: This really depends on what age your mates are. If they don't have kids then start mid-afternoon on a Sunday and plough on into the early evening. If they do, then the daytime option is probably best. That brings one little problem, though – an unhappy combination of kids and red wine. Take precautions (cover your sofas with old throws, have plenty of salt and stain removers handy, etc.) and act fast on spillages.

Other things you'll need: A ladle and jug to pour the mulled wine; napkins; glasses; oven gloves for offering the mince pies around when they've just come out of the oven.

With all that in place you should have a great time, so much so that by the following autumn your mates will be demanding to know when there's going to be another one.

christmas

This should be a jolly season in the calendar, but it's all too often a time when the cook of the house cracks up because of a combination of two things: too much ambition and too little organization. Too much ambition will see you preparing five types of stuffing, four different vegetable dishes, three helpings of meat, two sauces, and perhaps even a partridge in a pear tree. Too little organization will mean you are exhausted on Christmas Day, having to run around like a headless chicken at the last minute. To make the festive season as painless as possible, here's a handy list of things that you need to do in the run-up to Christmas, and dates you should aim to do them by.

Christmas pudding and cake: Make these at the same time in **mid-November** since they're very similar recipes, with the exception that one also uses suet (if you don't know which, here's a little suggestion – perhaps you should get someone else to do Christmas). Keep in a cool place and water liberally with brandy – the cake and pudding that is, not you.

Check the decorations: Also in **mid-November** you should dig out the Christmas tree decorations to make sure that the lights work and that the baubles haven't cracked. If anything's not quite right you then have plenty of time to get replacements so that your decorations can be up on **1 December**.

Ordering the meat: Have a word with your butcher towards the **end of November** about when it's best to order the meat.

Plan your menu: Not everyone enjoys roast turkey, Brussels sprouts and Christmas pudding. Christmas lunch is a meal which includes lots of things that people don't really eat throughout the rest of the year, so check what your guests like by **early December**. Set a deadline for them to reply, so that you have all the info at your fingertips in time for your meat-ordering deadline. If there'll be a veggie around the table, practise some meat-free options.

Buy in the booze: Get this out of the way by **early December**, unless you or other family members can't be trusted with booze in the house, in which case leave it until Christmas Eve. Remember to cater for other people's drinking choices – super-strength lager might be your favourite tipple, but don't even think of feeding it to your granddad as he's either going to pass out or think he's Shakin' Stevens and start performing during lunch. When you're checking on the food also ask about the booze, otherwise you'll buy lager when your brother-in-law only drinks bitter. Don't forget a bottle or two for mulled wine, and soft drinks. Lemonade's a good choice for slipping into your nan's hand and pretending it's a G&T when she's had one too many.

Your meat order: This should go in **three weeks before** Christmas or thereabouts, as you should know everyone's foodie likes and dislikes by now. Don't forget, unless you want to be picking up a frozen turkey from Iceland on Christmas Eve and praying it defrosts in time.

Glassware, cutlery, crockery: You're catering for more people than usual, so **three weeks before** check you have enough of everything, and buy or borrow extra if needed.

Seating: If it's your debut Christmas as host or you've just moved home, then you could well be having more people sitting around your table than you've ever had before. **Three weeks before**, count up how many seats you have (and check whether your table's big enough to cope with the full family gathering), and if you don't have enough then make arrangements to borrow them.

Icing the cake: The marzipan is the first layer and can be done as early as **two weeks before**, as long as you keep the cake in an airtight container. Don't forget that real marzipan is made from raw eggs, so have another cake option handy if any pregnant women are coming round. Add the icing layer a couple of days later.

Mince pies: Assuming you've either skipped the mulled wine and mince pie party or have none left over, make these **two weeks before** if you're able to freeze them.

Visit the pharmacist: Someone will over-indulge: it's the second law of Christmas (the first being that the kids will get up at 5am). **One week before**, buy indigestion tablets for that bloated belly, painkillers to cope with the cricked neck you get after passing out in front of the telly, plus aspirin for the morning after the night before.

Don't forget non-perishables: Unless you're a masochist and want to brave the supermarkets much closer to Christmas, buy in the non-perishables **one week before** at the latest. Don't forget all those things which aren't necessarily festive, but which you can't do without on the big day: toilet roll, coffee, tea, cereal, foil, tonic water, sugar.

Launder all your table linen: This is a job to get out of the way by **20 December** – by then you probably won't need them again before the big day, but you shouldn't end up forgetting to wash them as you get distracted by more important matters in those vital last couple of days before Christmas.

Timetable the big day: Start thinking about when you need to cook everything and have this fully worked out by **21 December** – that way the day should run smoothly. Also decide which jobs other people can do to help, and give everyone something to do (unless you're a control freak in which case, good luck).

Pick up the meat: Do this by **Christmas Eve** at the latest, if not by **23 December**. And if there are two or more hosts, don't assume that someone else will do it. Be sure to check (or risk eating Spam for Christmas Day lunch!).

Shop for perishables: You'll have to leave this until **23 December** or even **Christmas Eve**. Whichever day you choose, shop as early in the morning as possible. If you're shopping online, book your delivery slot well in advance or risk missing out. Alternatively, try an organic vegetable box scheme, especially if it supplies other provisions like milk, cheese, fish and meat for Boxing Day and beyond.

Make the stuffing: Do this on **Christmas Eve**, as well as defrosting the mince pies and setting the table if you can. Then it's all down to the big day, which should go smoothly because you've planned everything in advance.

Classic Christmas cock-ups
Here are some classic mistakes to avoid on Christmas Day.

Over-sleeping: You've enjoyed a convivial Christmas Eve, you've been off work for a couple of days so aren't used to setting the alarm, and you wake up at noon … which means no food before 6pm.

Over-indulging: You decide to join everyone for a glass of champers, and then another. Suddenly it's all getting a bit hazy and the turkey's cooked but the spuds aren't even on. Oh dear. Or perhaps you could end up kissing goodbye to pudding, as *Loose*

Women panellist Sherrie Hewson did when she dropped hers on Celebrity Christmas *Come Dine With Me* – although she scooped it back on to the plate, her guests weren't exactly desperate to eat it.

Frozen turkey: The best place for the bird to defrost is in the fridge but that takes time, so make sure you work out exactly how long it will need.

Lousy time-keeping: Make a note of when different dishes go on to cook, otherwise it'll be impossible to work out when everything's ready.

Dodgy table-setting: Don't concentrate so hard on dinner that you forget salt, pepper, water, crackers, serving spoons and sauces for the table, otherwise you'll constantly be jumping up from the table and delaying the start of the meal.

Wine woes: Don't just focus on the food: remember to chill the white wine and to fetch that red from the garage so that it can warm up.

Don't be a martyr: As the host you should also be able to enjoy yourself, so take some of the strain out of the day by allocating a few jobs to your guests.

Nightmare with nibbles: Too many pre-dinner crisps results in left-over spuds and sprouts; too few and all that festive champers goes to everyone's heads.

Don't forget people's food dislikes: You might have cooked a veggie main course, but it's all too easy to slap on all the meaty accompaniments without thinking. This happened to Sunderland contestant Roy Ledger on *Come Dine With Me* when he put pigs in blankets on Bernice Saltzer's plate, forgetting that she didn't eat bacon.

Scissor scares: Don't use them to enthusiastically open over-wrapped presents: 80,000 souls end up in A&E on Christmas Day after scissor mishaps!

boxing day

It's the end of Christmas Day: your father-in-law is snoozing off his lunch on the sofa, the kids are already fighting over whose turn it is on the Wii, the recycling bin looks as if you've just played host to a rock star's birthday party, and your stomach is bulging at the seams.

And there's still Boxing Day to come ... You contemplate doing it all over again – more roasties, more pud, more brandy butter – but don't even think about it. If you can't stop yourself thinking about it, then listen to your stomach groaning – that should tell you it's a bad idea.

Boxing Day is another chance to get together with family and friends, but no one will appreciate another big feast. Think light meals, anything easy on the stomach and served without stuffing. This is a chance to be kind to your local fishmonger – after all, he doesn't stock turkey so he's facing a bit of a hiding. Help him out by choosing a fish dish on Boxing Day. Buy some in advance and pop it in the freezer ready for defrosting on Christmas night – assuming you're not so befuddled with drink (and/or depressed by the miserable *EastEnders'* Christmas storyline) that you forget.

The ultimate easy way out is to do cold meats, jacket potatoes and pickles. It's a pleasant alternative to richer food, and you can still make it Christmassy with a few left-over mince pies. Whatever you do, don't do turkey curry.

The Boxing Day drinks party

Mention a Boxing Day drinks party and anyone who knows *Bridget Jones* will think Christmas jumpers, mad uncles and warring parents. On the other hand, if you stage a successful party then your guests will love you for getting them out of the house, and for taking the pressure off their own catering!). However, this comes with the same problem as the mulled wine party – once you do it successfully, everyone expects their invitation as soon as the clocks go back.

But don't dismiss it entirely out of hand. Here are a few reasons why it can be a good idea.

- It's a way of bringing different sides of the family together (that might not be a good idea for everyone, but I like to think there's merit in it) without having to cook for loads and loads of people.
- Most people want to carry on celebrating Christmas but are a bit bored of the idea of sitting down for another dinner.
- You get to use up all those left-over peanuts, crisps and sweets.
- You don't have to speak to the people who you spent Christmas Day with, which can be a bonus in some households!

Here are a few ways to cope with the party.

- Think ahead and buy your wine from an off-licence which also provides free glasses. Majestic is one chain that does it – you pay a deposit which you get back as long as you return them clean and intact. Chances are they will also do sale or return above a minimum order, which can help the Christmas budget. Pick the right place and they'll even deliver both for you.
- If you want food, prepare a buffet – preferably of stuff that you have already cooked up and stored in the freezer, such as quiches, lasagnes and moussakas. Stock up so that you don't have to venture out of the house. The shops might be open on Boxing Day, but who really wants to be at the supermarket, surrounded by marked-down Christmas puddings? Your guests, stuffed with rich food from the day before, won't be expecting cordon bleu cooking, so treat them to simpler stuff.
- Canapés are great in theory, but they need time, patience and lots of willing hands to make enough, so think long and hard about these. It's probably best to choose just a few simple ones that you can offer up before the buffet hits the table.
- Be upfront with the drinks: if you've been battling away in the kitchen the day before, you shouldn't

be running around on Boxing Day serving people. Tell everyone as soon as they arrive to help themselves, and make it easier by having a table with the wine and a couple of corkscrews on. You could even have wine already poured out in glasses.

- For the music, avoid the Christmas CD – everyone will be bored of it as they will have heard it in the shops since the beginning of October.
- Timing-wise, it's probably best to host the party from lunchtime until late afternoon. Don't be afraid of being blatant if people are over-staying their welcome. Start clearing away plates or filling the dishwasher, or, if they really don't get the hint, put the telly on – that'll drive them away.
- Then there's the question of who to invite: family, friends or neighbours? Choose whoever takes your fancy, but make sure they're all reliable and that they will turn up. Otherwise, if only a handful do, you'll have wasted all that time and effort for nothing.
- Make sure you have more non-alcoholic drinks than normal – it won't just be the drivers drinking them, but also those with Christmas hangovers.
- For those who have over-indulged, have a few hair-of-the-dog cocktails to hand: Bloody Mary is a great one that you can just mix up in a jug and leave for people to tuck into.

new year's eve

This can be one of the most expensive times of the year, but there's no reason why you can't tuck into some good food at home with your mates and still go out and enjoy the party atmosphere afterwards.

If you do intend to go out after dinner, here are a few suggestions on how to plan the party.

- Start promptly and be organized: that way you're more likely to get to your chosen venue in time and not have to queue as if you're at the first day of the Harrods' January sale. Ask your guests to arrive on time for the same reason.

- Stick to just two courses: that way you will ensure a swift getaway, plus New Year's Eve is about partying – a few drinks, a dance – so people won't want to be stuffed full of food.
- You've been cooking away all Christmas, so spread the load – you can do the main, someone else can bring a side dish that you can stick in the oven (potato gratin often fits the bill) and someone else can do the starter or dessert.
- Make sure you have lots of mirrors – the ladies will want to do their make-up and check their hair, and if they're all trying to peek into the same mirror then the taxi you booked will come and go, and you'll be getting public transport to the venue because it's impossible to order another one.

new year's eve away from home

This is a great idea for families with kids – it's exciting, you all get away, you all get to cook together. But just like holidaying with mates, it's fraught with potential problems. Someone's a bit tight and is always checking what you spend; you forget your mates' allergies; you forget to cater for everyone's kids . . .

So avoid the pitfalls and plan, plan, plan. Agree a menu in advance, and decide who's going to buy what. It could be the person with the massive car and the fewest kids, or the person who's likely to get there first.

You could of course blag it on the day . . . if you like wasting your precious holiday time coming to some sort of agreement about what to eat, then shopping for it, then going to another shop because you can't find all the ingredients. But what's the point of booking a cottage with a roaring log fire if you spend no time in front of it?

Since not everyone has the same budget, be realistic in what you're cooking. Similarly, be realistic with the price tag for your wine, especially since you don't want to be stingy with the quantity. If you're too scared to get tipsy in front of the in-laws over Christmas, a get-together with friends could well be the first time you've had the opportunity to really let your hair down, so there's a good chance you'll start drinking early. But remember there's nothing worse than starting to feel the effects of a hangover as the clock strikes midnight because the booze ran out two hours earlier and you're stuck in the middle of nowhere, so make sure you bring plenty. After all, if there's any left, you'll be more than happy drinking it during those long, cold nights in January and February.

Decide who's going to cook, but don't always accept the first volunteer: friends who think they're great cooks often aren't (after all, where would *Come Dine With Me* be without people like that?). To avoid the unwanted volunteer cooking, decide between the rest of you who will cook instead and then tell the unwanted volunteer that it's too late, you've already decided who's doing what. Or better still, agree among yourselves who does what best, and allocate the different courses accordingly. Whichever way you decide, after all the preparation that's involved with Christmas Day, make New Year's Eve easy for yourself by sharing the load as much as possible.

valentine's day

Dining out is the easy (and expensive) option. However, it often seems as if there are only three types of couples who dine out on 14 February: the ones who are all over each other, kissing, cooing and generally looking like they should get a room; the couples who are on the verge of breaking up, but with one half hoping that a really expensive meal, followed by flowers and chocolates, will patch things up; and the ones who have nothing to say to each other.

However well you plan your date, there's a good chance you'll end up sitting next to one of these couples, or possibly all three. Plus the restaurant will have jammed in some extra tables because it's the one night when they cash in, so you can hear everything – the stony silence on your left, the cooing and smooching on your right, and the arguing just behind you. All of these combine to make an evening at home all the more attractive.

Plus what could be more romantic than cooking a three-course meal, whether it's for a loved one or a new date? Just remember, this isn't just any old meal, but one that comes fraught with hidden meaning.

The new date
Choosing the menu: If you've been dating for a bit and reckon that tonight is the night, then tagliatelle primavera followed by beef Wellington and sponge pudding means that the best you can probably hope for is a peck on the cheek before your date asks you to pass the indigestion tablets.

On the other hand, a menu of oysters followed by asparagus, more seafood and a chocolatey pudding – all reckoned to be aphrodisiacs – will look a little too obvious, so get the balance right.

Also be mindful of the time you have, as the odds are that Valentine's Day will fall on a work night. A three-course menu is great, but a three-course menu cooked entirely in the hour before your date arrives? Now that requires skill.

Choose a menu with at least one course which you can do in advance and two others that you can stick in the oven while you try out your witty banter. Actually, that's not good advice: while you try to make polite conversation.

Your date will know if you've been working all day so they won't think there's much of a dinner in store if they turn up and you have nothing left to do. Instead, choose a menu that takes at least an hour and five minutes to prepare. You get home at 6.30pm and have half an hour to get ready, with an hour of preparation time before the big arrival at eight. If you have everything done by 7.55pm and you're sitting on the sofa with a smug look on your face when they arrive, it will look like you've not made quite enough effort, so those last five minutes are vital – if you keep them standing in the kitchen for just a few moments while you fix them a drink and finish off one last job, then it looks like you've gone to lots of effort. But equally don't overrun, otherwise you'll commit the fatal Valentine's Day sin of leaving them sitting on the sofa alone for ages while you do a very sweaty impression of Gordon Ramsay as you battle with a fish cake that won't form properly.

Try to do some subtle research on your date's likes and dislikes. The more you can do without them knowing, the more chance you'll have of impressing them. If you don't bother and your first course is mushroom soup served to a mushroom-hater then you're done for.

Don't be afraid to buy in tricky stuff for the end of the meal – chocolate truffles, for instance – but if you're going to do canapés, do them yourself. They're the first thing your date will eat, and if they recognize them as the same ones they bought in Marks & Spencer the other weekend, then you're scuppered before you've even started. The food which follows may well be a celebration of home-cooking – with jus, reductions, foams, coulis and all those other cheffy things – but none of it will dislodge that bad first impression. Bought chocolate truffles are fine though, since by that stage you should (if it's all gone to plan) have already impressed with three courses of marvellous food.

If it's a menu you haven't done before, practise. Whatever you do, don't get someone in to do it for you. Even if they disappear before your date arrives, they may well leave clues behind them, and you'll come across as a bit of a sneaky one.

Also do a bit of research on the drinks your beau or belle enjoys – champagne seems to be the obvious choice, but not everyone likes it. If you want the evening to feel particularly romantic, it's best to plump for wine over beer.

The night before: Choose your music. This might sound silly but, just like choosing the menu, it's all about creating the right atmosphere. The right atmosphere isn't putting on 'Barry White's Greatest Hits' when your date arrives, which is too unsubtle, nor is it some thrash metal album, which is too much like making the contrary point. Choose a selection of songs that work; better still do a play list on your iPod and have it already plugged into your speakers.

On the day: In the morning, get up early and do a few things before heading out to work: set the table, put out the candles, check you have matches, put the champagne in the fridge, prepare your pud. If you're a boy, check the toilet – and in all likelihood that means clean it. If you're a girl, lay out your outfit – and make a vow to stick to that choice, as any dithering when you return home means less time to cook before your date arrives, then even more panic when he does.

At work, don't fall foul of the first law of 14 February: the curse of the single boss. Bachelor or spinster, young or old, they will have a special Valentine's Day antenna which ensures they know that you're going on a date. They will keep you busy with those very uninteresting accounts, so there's only one solution: get your strike in first. A doctor's appointment, toothache, a sick gran in hospital – use anything to get you out of the office on time.

Before you leave, check on your transport home and know your alternative routes. Otherwise, prepare to fall foul of sod's law: if you have a reason to get home on time, public transport will fail you without exception. You wouldn't want to spend your life as a singleton, wondering what might have been, just because you didn't check and got stuck on the train for an hour.

Like all dinner parties, make a clear plan for your timings otherwise you're scuppered.

If you're a guy hosting the meal, don't ask your date to take her shoes off when she arrives. You might have a spanking new white carpet, it might be pouring down outside, but a woman's footwear is as much a part of her outfit as her clothes. She'll have spent time agonizing over which shoes work with that dress, so don't mess it all up – and leave her feeling a bit deflated – by asking her to go barefoot. It would be like her asking you to take your shirt off, so don't mention the shoes (except to say how nice they are).

The other awkward thing on arrival is whether or not you exchange presents: if you've bought one and your date hasn't, they'll feel embarrassed, so it's probably best to keep it back until later, once you've relaxed into the date.

If you're a guy buying for a girl, then think beyond chocolate and remember that perfume is only an option if you know what she likes. Instead, buy something that involves a bit of research: for instance, discreetly find out what her favourite beauty products are. And discreet means not asking her best mate because, girls being girls, they'll talk and then your surprise won't be a surprise for long. Plus, if you've failed to buy the discussed gift because you paid the electricity bill instead, she'll be bitterly disappointed.

If it's the other way round, try to work out your man's favourite sport and maybe get a match ticket, or tickets for a concert if he's more musically inclined. Again, discreetly check out what he likes – but make sure you do it in good time to get the right tickets.

From then on, it's down to you and your best-laid plans, so get cooking and good luck.

The long-term partner

It's not just new lovebirds who take note of Valentine's Day: there are those who are single, and those in a long-term relationship.

If you're single, just ignore the date: go to the cinema, or have a drink with mates in a pub (it'll be full of other singletons, so you never know, you might get lucky). Whatever you do, don't throw a dinner party for your single friends. Someone will drink too much and get maudlin that they haven't got a partner, and you'll spend half the night comforting them.

For the longer-term couple, Valentine's Day usually evokes two very contrasting responses: 'We celebrate our love every day of the year, so we don't need to be told when to do it' or, 'It's a real chance to devote a day to us and our relationship; we love it.'

If you're in the former camp, don't bother reading on. If one of you is in each camp, then you've probably already come to a long-standing agreement about what to do on Valentine's Day. If you're in the latter camp then the trick is keeping it fresh, as you've probably been celebrating in the same house, with the same candlesticks, for a good few years now.

Here are a few ideas on how to still make it a night to remember.

- Each year take turns to cook, so that you both look forward to the chance to impress.
- Ban your other half from the house until dinner. Make them get ready at a friend's house so that it feels like a real date.
- Agree to buy each other presents, but don't do anything obvious.
- Cook something you've never cooked before.
- Drink something that you never normally drink – go to an off-licence and get some wine tips once you've decided on your menu.
- Buy some new table dressings on a regular basis, so that you have plenty to choose from.
- Wear an outfit which your other half hasn't seen before.
- Play music that brings back happy memories.
- Round off the evening with a few photos of your favourite moments of your life together.
- Book a babysitter. Even better, send the kids for an overnight stay with their favourite aunt!
- Best of all, get away from home (and the kids, if you can find relatives to look after them) by hiring a nifty little self-catering cottage or apartment, so that it can feel like a real break.

canapés, amuse-bouches & starters

Dan Redfern

oysters with shallot vinegar

4 oysters, as fresh as possible
crushed ice
about 20g seaweed
4 lemon wedges

FOR THE SHALLOT VINEGAR
20ml red wine
20ml red wine vinegar
1 shallot, finely chopped

SERVES FOUR

I'm a big fish fanatic, so oysters were an obvious starter. The oysters were the most unusual part of my meal - they are a real explosion of taste. I always smell them before serving to check they are a hundred per cent fresh - you'll know if they're not.

1 Mix the ingredients for the shallot vinegar in a bowl.

2 Open the oysters with an oyster shucker - watch your fingers! Disconnect the oysters from their shells and lay them back in place. Discard the top shells.

3 Arrange the oysters on a bed of crushed ice with the seaweed and lemon wedges.

4 Drizzle each oyster with as much shallot vinegar as you fancy - and down the hatch. I like to chew, others prefer to swallow in one.

Oliver Gillie

stilton soufflés with smoked haddock salad

25g unsalted butter, plus extra for greasing
25g plain flour
250ml milk
75g cheese (a mixture of crumbled Stilton and grated Cheddar is good)
3 medium egg yolks
pinch of cayenne pepper
pinch of mustard powder
5 medium egg whites
25g Stilton cheese, crumbled
100ml double cream

FOR THE SALAD
300g smoked haddock fillets
250ml milk
1 x 250g pack baby lettuce leaves
extra virgin olive oil
balsamic vinegar

SERVES SIX
I am a great believer in soufflés, as they are much easier than most people think and taste delicious even when they 'fail'. Whatever you do, use plenty of egg whites! Any combination of cheese is fine, too.

1 Preheat the oven to 200°C/Gas 6. Butter 6 x 200ml soufflé dishes or ramekins. Cover a baking sheet with non-stick baking parchment.

2 Melt the butter in a saucepan on medium heat, add the flour and stir to form a roux. Cook for 1 minute, stirring, then remove from the heat and gradually add the milk, whisking vigorously after each addition. Return to the heat and bring to the boil, stirring, then simmer for about 2 minutes until thickened and smooth. Remove from the heat and cool slightly, then stir in the 75g mixed cheese followed by the egg yolks, cayenne, mustard and seasoning to taste.

3 Using electric beaters, whisk the egg whites to stiff peaks in a large bowl. Now slowly and gently fold the egg whites into the sauce mixture until evenly incorporated.

4 Spoon the mixture into the soufflé dishes, then run the tip of a sharp knife around the edge of each soufflé to release it from the side of the dish (this will help the soufflés rise). Pour cold water into the roasting tin to come halfway up the sides of the dishes. Bake for 20 minutes or until the soufflés are well risen and golden on top, with a slight wobble in the centre when shaken.

5 Allow the soufflés to cool until they collapse, then loosen around the edges with a palette knife and turn them out, placing them the right way up on the lined baking sheet.

6 Put the Stilton and cream into a small pan and heat gently, stirring, until the Stilton has melted. Place 2 spoonfuls of this creamy mix on top of each soufflé and bake for 10–15 minutes until risen again.

7 Meanwhile, put the haddock into a shallow pan with the milk and bring to a gentle simmer. Cover and poach for 5 minutes or until the fish flakes easily with a fork. Drain the fish well and discard any skin and bones.

8 To serve, arrange a bed of lettuce on each of 6 plates. Drizzle with oil and vinegar and top with the fish. Place a soufflé next to the salad and serve at once.

Mike Aldous

fillets of sea bass with sun-dried tomato risotto

5 sea bass fillets, skin on
1 tbsp olive oil

FOR THE RISOTTO
2 tbsp olive oil
4 shallots, finely sliced
2 sticks celery, trimmed and diced
1 clove garlic, finely chopped
150g risotto rice
50ml dry white wine
850–900ml hot fish stock
25g Parmesan cheese, freshly grated
8 sun-dried tomatoes, drained and chopped
2 tbsp chopped fresh herbs, such as
  parsley, dill and chives

SERVES FIVE

This dish is fit for any occasion (we designed it for our wedding breakfast). Your guests will be proper impressed and it's a cinch. The secret is to quickly fry the dry ingredients, then flood with white wine and stock. Then stir, stir, stir. Enjoy stirring the risotto with a large glass of something, and serve with a chilled Sauvignon Blanc.

1 Pat the fish fillets dry with kitchen paper and score the skin on each fish a couple of times with a sharp knife. Set aside.

2 Make the risotto. Heat the olive oil in a large saucepan and gently fry the shallots, celery and garlic on low to medium heat for 5–8 minutes until soft, stirring occasionally. Add the rice and cook for a further minute, stirring regularly, then add the wine and stir until it is all absorbed.

3 Now start to add the hot stock gradually to the pan a ladleful at a time, stirring well after each addition and adjusting the heat under the pan if necessary. Don't add more stock until the previous amount has been absorbed. Stir the rice often and cook for about 18 minutes or until soft, tender and creamy.

4 Ten minutes before the rice is ready, season the fish with salt and pepper on both sides. Heat a large non-stick frying pan on medium to high heat. Pour in the olive oil and heat until hot, then add the fish fillets and cook for 3 minutes on each side, starting skin-side down.

5 Remove the risotto from the heat and stir in the Parmesan and tomatoes. Season to taste with salt and pepper. Spoon on to 5 warmed plates and top each serving with a sea bass fillet, placed skin-side up. Sprinkle with the herbs and serve at once.

Richard Carpenter

smoked salmon soda breads

5 heaped tbsp crème fraîche
2–3 tsp hot horseradish sauce, to taste
about 50g pickled red cabbage, well drained
175–200g very thinly sliced smoked salmon,
   cut into small pieces
5 slices brown soda bread

This recipe for salmon soda breads is very easy to do –
we sometimes get the kids to do it! The day before you
can cut the soda breads and seal in a plastic bag, and
mix the horseradish and crème fraîche then leave in the
fridge, then simply assemble them just before the party.

1 Mix the crème fraîche in a bowl with horseradish sauce
to taste.

2 Chop the pickled cabbage into small pieces (scissors are
good for this) and cut the salmon slices into strips.

3 Cut the crusts off the bread and square off the ends,
then cut each slice into 4 x 4cm squares so that you have
20 squares altogether.

4 Spread the crème fraîche mixture over the bread,
arrange the smoked salmon on top and finish with the
red cabbage.

Harinder Khela

quorn tikka wraps with cool mint raita

4 tortilla wraps
iceberg lettuce, finely chopped

FOR THE RAITA
1 x 150g carton plain yoghurt
2–3 tsp mint sauce (from a jar)

FOR THE FILLING
2 tbsp vegetable oil
1 onion, sliced
½ tsp cumin seeds
½ tsp salt
1 x 350g pack Quorn chunks
1 tsp dried fenugreek leaves
1 tsp chopped fresh chilli (with or without
    seeds according to taste)
½ tsp tandoori masala mix
4 heaped tbsp tikka paste

SERVES EIGHT

A hot Mexican dish with an exotic Indian twist – who could resist? These look and taste as if you've spent hours preparing them, but actually they're really simple to make. For those who can't stand the heat, the raita really cools these down – so no need to stay out of the kitchen. I use Quorn because it adds texture and soaks up the flavours, but if you're a hardened carnivore you could use chicken if you really wanted to.

1 Make the raita by mixing the yoghurt in a bowl with mint sauce to taste. Cover and keep in the fridge until ready to serve.

2 Make the filling. Heat the oil in a deep frying pan until hot and fry the onion for a few minutes on medium heat until softened and translucent. Add the cumin seeds and salt and stir-fry for a minute or two, then add the Quorn and cook for 5 minutes, stirring occasionally until starting to colour. Now add the remaining ingredients and cook on low to medium heat for a further 5 minutes, stirring often and moistening with about 6 tbsp water to prevent the mixture from becoming too thick.

3 Divide the filling equally among the 4 tortillas, spooning it along the centre. Top with lettuce and raita, roll the tortillas around the filling and cut each one in half on the diagonal. Serve straightaway.

Vanessa Boukharouba

coquilles saint-jacques

18 scallops, plus 6 scrubbed scallop shells
   if you can get them
75g butter
150g mushrooms, finely chopped
1 shallot, finely chopped
25g plain flour
150ml dry white wine
150ml fish stock
1–2 tbsp crème fraîche
1 medium egg yolk
2 tbsp finely chopped fresh flat-leaf parsley
2 tsp finely chopped fresh chives
6 tbsp fresh white breadcrumbs
6 tbsp grated Parmesan cheese

SERVES SIX

As is typically French, a posh name for a simple yet effective starter. Ensure the scallops are poached gently or they will only be good for bouncing off walls! Serve in scallop shells for that 1980s dinner-party twist.

1 Preheat the oven to 220°C/Gas 7.

2 Pull off and discard the tough, crescent-shaped muscle on the side of each scallop. Lower the scallops into a pan of simmering water, using a large slotted spoon. Wait until the water returns to a simmer, then poach the scallops gently for 1 minute only. Remove with the slotted spoon and drain on kitchen paper.

3 Melt 25g of the butter in a frying pan on medium heat until just sizzling. Add the mushrooms and shallot and fry, stirring often, for about 5 minutes until the mushrooms are soft and most of their liquid has been driven off.

4 Add 25g of the remaining butter to the pan. When it starts to foam, add the flour and stir for 1 minute. Gradually pour in the wine and stock, whisking constantly after each addition. Bring to the boil, stirring, and simmer for 2 minutes. Remove from the heat and leave to cool slightly before stirring in the crème fraîche, egg yolk, herbs and salt and pepper to taste.

5 Place 3 scallops in each of 6 scallop shells or individual baking dishes and spoon over the sauce. Sprinkle with the breadcrumbs and Parmesan and dot with the remaining butter. Bake for 10 minutes, or until golden and bubbling. Serve hot.

Gary Holden

french onion soup with gruyère croûtes

50g butter
1kg white onions, thinly sliced
3 bay leaves
½ bunch fresh thyme, tied with string
½ head garlic, cut crossways
20g plain flour
375ml dry white wine
200ml port
1 x 400g can beef consommé
700–900ml good beef stock

FOR THE CROÛTES

5 slices baguette
2 cloves garlic, cut in half
2 tbsp Dijon mustard
100g Gruyère cheese, grated

SERVES FIVE

This dish reminds me of a holiday some years ago, and as far as I remember this recipe comes close to that first experience. The key to this dish is to cook it and then simmer it for as long as possible, but don't let it reduce too much! It seems as if there's a lot of booze in it, but, trust me, it won't have any effect on your ability to host a successful dinner party! Use a good-quality stock (a shop-bought one will do the trick).

1 Melt the butter in a large saucepan and fry the onions on low heat for about 10 minutes until translucent, stirring occasionally. Add the bay leaves, thyme and garlic, increase the heat to medium and continue frying, stirring frequently, until the onions are golden brown. This will take about 10 minutes.

2 Sprinkle the flour over the onions and cook, stirring, for 2 minutes. Pour in the white wine, stir to mix with the onions, then boil for about 10 minutes until reduced by about half. Now add the port and reduce again.

3 Pour in the consommé and 700ml stock, season to taste with salt and pepper and bring to the boil on high heat. Lower the heat to medium and simmer for about 20 minutes until the onions are very soft and the liquid has reduced slightly. At this stage you can adjust the consistency to your liking by adding more stock and simmering for a few minutes more. Remove the bay leaves, thyme and garlic, taste for seasoning and keep hot until ready to serve.

4 For the croûtes, preheat the grill on medium-high setting. Toast the slices on both sides, then rub one side with a cut side of the garlic and spread with mustard. Top with the cheese and grill for 3–4 minutes until melted.

5 Ladle the soup into 5 warmed bowls and top each one with a croûte. Serve immediately, before the bread has a chance to soften too much.

Milly Johnson

black pudding with goat's cheese & honey-balsamic glaze

5 potato scones
5 slices good-quality black pudding
   (the leanest possible)
1 beefsteak tomato, cut into 5 slices
5 slices goat's cheese

TO SERVE
green salad leaves
2 tbsp runny honey
2 tbsp balsamic vinegar

I invented this concoction because it's got a wonderful and varied selection of flavours to it, plus if you leave off the salad – and add an egg – it's a perfect breakfast dish too. It's also a nice fusion of my Scottish and Yorkshire roots with the 'tatty scone' base under the pudding. I had my pudding specially made with no fat but extra spice to compensate for the taste (a good butcher will 'customize' it for you). If your guests aren't brave enough to try the black pudding, or you need a vegetarian option, scrap the pudding and just enjoy the other flavours.

1 Preheat the grill on medium-high setting. Grill the potato scones and black pudding on both sides, about 5 minutes in total.

2 Place a slice of tomato on top of each potato scone and a slice of goat's cheese on each slice of black pudding. Grill until the tomato softens and the cheese is slightly runny, about 5 minutes again.

3 Meanwhile, make a small bed of salad on 5 plates. Warm the honey and balsamic vinegar in a small pan, stirring to mix.

4 To serve, place the potato scone and tomato in the centre of the salad and top with the black pudding and cheese. Drizzle the warm dressing sparingly over the whole dish, just to give a hint of flavour.

Wayne Hinds

poached egg over black pudding & bacon with rocket salad

8 rashers cured streaky bacon
8 slices black pudding
1 tbsp malt or wine vinegar
4 eggs, preferably bantam

FOR THE SALAD
1 x 100g bag rocket salad
extra virgin olive oil
balsamic vinegar

SERVES FOUR

I chose this recipe for several reasons: it is very simple to prepare and, apart from the black pudding which can easily be omitted, who can resist bacon and egg? We have our own chickens and there is nothing quite like fresh free-range eggs, especially as we have bantams, which lay tiny eggs that are perfect for a starter. This recipe is so basic that the quality of the ingredients is all-important: salad from the garden if possible, home-cured bacon from your local butcher, and of course the best-quality, local black pudding.

1 Preheat the grill on medium-high setting.

2 Grill the bacon and black pudding for about 10 minutes until the bacon is crisp, turning the pieces over halfway.

3 Meanwhile, toss the rocket salad in a large bowl with a drizzle each of olive oil and balsamic vinegar and salt and pepper to taste. Divide the salad between 4 plates.

4 Now poach the eggs. Fill a wide, shallow pan two-thirds full with water, add the vinegar and bring to a simmer on high heat. Crack the eggs one at a time into a small bowl, then slide into the water and turn the heat down low. Simmer for 3 minutes, remove with a slotted spoon and drain.

5 Remove the bacon and black pudding from the grill, drain briefly on kitchen paper, then place on individual plates with the dressed salad and poached eggs. Slice through the yolks, grind a little black pepper over them and serve at once, with the yolks running.

Javine
sticky ribs

4 racks of baby back pork ribs
   (about 16 ribs in total)
vegetable oil

FOR THE MARINADE
1 onion, chopped
4 cloves garlic, chopped
2 tbsp tomato purée
2 tbsp soy sauce
1 tbsp Worcestershire sauce
2 tbsp soft brown sugar

SERVES FOUR

This is a family favourite of mine. As the name implies, this is a sticky and messy dish! Full of rich, sweet, aromatic flavour, it can be served as a starter with a garnish, or as a main course with noodles or rice. The ribs are marinated overnight so they can just be thrown into the oven, leaving you to relax while the aromas tease your guests!

1 Cut the pork into individual ribs and place in a single layer in an ovenproof dish.

2 Whiz all the marinade ingredients in a blender or food processor to make a runny purée.

3 Pour the marinade over the ribs and turn them until they are evenly coated. Cover with foil and leave to marinate in the fridge for 24 hours, bringing them to room temperature about 30 minutes before cooking.

4 Preheat the oven to 180°C/Gas 4.

5 Uncover the ribs and roast for 30 minutes.

6 After 30 minutes increase the oven temperature to 200°C/Gas 6. Turn the ribs over and continue roasting for 1 hour, turning them over 2–3 times more and drizzling with oil about halfway through. The ribs are ready when they are dark brown and sizzling. Serve hot, with finger bowls and plenty of paper napkins.

Stuart Hudson
rabbit terrine

12 rashers unsmoked streaky bacon
30g butter
1 onion, finely chopped
1 large clove garlic, finely chopped
250g chicken livers, bitter white
    filaments removed
2 tbsp brandy
pinch of freshly grated nutmeg
1 tsp Dijon mustard
a few fresh sage leaves, chopped
600g boneless rabbit, diced

TO SERVE
6 fresh figs, chopped
bread rolls or toast

For the show I wanted to use good local ingredients, and I'd recently had an amazing rabbit terrine at a restaurant near where I live. Be sure to chill it overnight to stop it from crumbling.

1 Preheat the oven to 170°C/Gas 3. Line a 1-litre terrine mould or loaf tin with the bacon, letting the rashers overhang the edges (I like to do this in an irregular pattern rather than the 'stripy' method).

2 Melt the butter in a deep frying pan and fry the onion and garlic on low to medium heat until softened but not browned. Remove with a slotted spoon.

3 Add the chicken livers to the pan and brown quickly on medium heat. At the same time, heat the brandy very gently in a small saucepan until just warmed through. Take the pan of chicken livers off the heat, pour the warm brandy over them and ignite with a long taper or match. Wait until the flames have died down completely, then stir in the softened onion and garlic with the nutmeg, mustard and sage. Leave to cool for 5 minutes or so.

4 Tip the contents of the pan into a blender and whiz to a smooth purée. Transfer the purée to a bowl and mix in the rabbit meat, then spoon the mixture into the bacon-lined terrine. Fold the overhanging bacon over the meat and top with extra pieces if there are any gaps. Cover with a piece of greaseproof paper, then foil.

5 Place the terrine in a roasting tin and pour in hot water to come halfway up the mould. Bake for 1¼ hours or until the terrine feels firm and has shrunk away slightly from the sides of the mould. When the terrine is cooked, remove from the oven and allow to cool.

6 Pour off any excess liquid, then cover the mould with a tray and place heavy weights on top. Chill in the fridge overnight.

7 To serve, remove the foil and greaseproof paper from the mould and turn the terrine out on to a board. Cut the terrine into 12 slices and arrange on 6 plates. Serve chilled, with the figs and bread rolls or toast.

main courses

Annette Evans

fillet of beef with roasted shallots

1 small bunch fresh rosemary
olive oil
3 cloves garlic, coarsely chopped
1.25kg fillet of beef, tied with string
12–18 shallots, peeled with root ends
    left intact

SERVES SIX

Although you can cook a really good piece of fillet without adding anything to it, this marinade makes it rather special. Combine the garlic, rosemary, salt and pepper, rub it into the meat and let it sit for a few hours or preferably overnight if you can – yum. This dish is easy to do and I think it's 'posh nosh'. Just be sure to buy quality ingredients.

1 Chop the needles from 2 of the rosemary sprigs and mix in a bowl with 2 tbsp olive oil, the garlic and black pepper to taste. Rub this mixture all over the beef, then tuck the remaining rosemary sprigs under the string. Set the beef aside at room temperature for at least 30 minutes. You can do this 24 hours ahead of time and keep the beef in the fridge, as long as you bring it to room temperature 1 hour before roasting.

2 Preheat the oven to 200°C/Gas 6.

3 Place the shallots in a roasting tin and drizzle with olive oil. Roast for 30 minutes or until soft and golden brown, shaking the tin occasionally to ensure even cooking.

4 Meanwhile, season the beef lightly with salt. Heat a splash of olive oil in another roasting tin until very hot and sear the beef until browned on all sides.

5 Place the beef in the oven and roast for 25 minutes for rare meat, 30 minutes for medium-rare. When the meat is done to your liking, take it out of the tin and leave to rest in a warm place for 10 minutes before serving with the roasted shallots.

Ian Jones
fillet steaks with crying pig sauce

2 tbsp rapeseed oil
6 rashers smoked streaky bacon (I like
    Gloucester Old Spot), rind removed and
    cut into lardons
2 large strong onions, roughly chopped (I find
    English organic are best for flavour if you
    can get them)
300ml beef stock
100ml brandy – a cheap, rough variety will do
100–150ml double cream
4 x 175g fillet steaks

Use good, strong cooking onions (crying), home-grown if possible, and dry cure bacon (pig) with plenty of booze (sauce). That's how I named it – simple!

1 Heat half the oil in a large, deep sauté pan until hot. Add the lardons and cook on low to medium heat until the fat runs, stirring frequently. Add the onions; sweat and colour them until they are tinged golden brown. This should take about 10 minutes, and you should stir frequently to prevent the onions from catching on the bottom of the pan.

2 Pour the stock into the pan. Increase the heat to high and boil the liquid hard, stirring frequently until it has reduced and just covers the onions. This should take about 5 minutes. Meanwhile, heat the brandy very gently in a small saucepan just until warmed through.

3 Remove the pan of onions from the heat, pour the warm brandy over them and ignite with a long taper or match. Wait until the flames have died down completely, then return the pan to the heat and finish off the sauce by stirring in 100ml cream and simmering gently for 2–3 minutes. Remove from the heat and set aside.

4 Brush the steaks with the remaining 1 tbsp oil and season with rock salt and freshly ground black pepper. Heat a griddle pan on high heat until very hot. Place the steaks on the pan, turn the heat down to medium and cook the steaks to your liking: 2–4 minutes on each side for rare to medium-rare meat. Remove the steaks from the pan and leave to rest in a warm place for 5 minutes.

5 Reheat the sauce if necessary, adding more cream if you like, then spoon over the steaks on 4 warmed plates. Serve straightaway.

Khakan Qureshi

chicken curry with pilau rice

125g butter or 125ml vegetable oil
4 onions, finely chopped
large knob of fresh root ginger, finely
    chopped or crushed
3–5 cloves garlic, finely chopped or crushed
3 green chillies, finely chopped (with or
    without seeds according to taste)
1 tsp cumin seeds
1 tsp salt
1 tsp chilli powder (medium, hot or extra hot)
1 tsp tandoori masala mix
1 tsp Madras curry powder (hot)
1 tsp turmeric
1 tsp paprika
2 tbsp plain yoghurt (optional)
1 x 400g can chopped tomatoes
4 skinless, boneless chicken breasts,
    cut into large chunks

FOR THE PILAU RICE
350g basmati rice (I always use Tilda)
125g butter
6 onions, finely chopped
6 cloves
6 black peppercorns
3 black cardamoms
3 bay leaves
1 tsp salt
about 900ml cold water

TO SERVE
1 tsp garam masala
2 tbsp chopped fresh coriander leaves
1 ripe tomato, finely chopped (optional)
2 red chillies, finely chopped with or without
    seeds according to taste (optional)

SERVES FOUR TO SIX

My recipe for chicken curry with pilau rice was inspired by my mother, Shamim Qureshi, who taught me how to cook it. Sadly, she passed away just before my programme was televised, so this is dedicated to her memory.

1 First prepare the rice for cooking. Wash and rinse it several times under cold running water until the water appears less cloudy. Place in a saucepan, cover generously with cold water and leave to soak for at least 1 hour.

2 For the curry, heat the butter in a large, non-stick flameproof casserole or saucepan on low to medium heat until foaming. Add the onions, ginger, garlic, chillies and cumin seeds, and fry until the mixture is very soft and golden brown, stirring frequently. This should take 25–30 minutes, and you may need to adjust the heat during this time.

3 Add the salt and all the spices, and stir well to mix with the onions. Now add the yoghurt, if using, and stir-fry for a few minutes until it is all absorbed – this will enhance the flavour of the curry and thicken the sauce. Stir in the tomatoes and half a can of water, bring to the boil on high heat, then simmer on medium heat for 15 minutes.

4 Place the chicken in the pan and mix well to coat in the sauce. Cover the pan and simmer gently on low to medium heat for 30 minutes or until the chicken is tender, stirring frequently to prevent the sauce sticking to the bottom of the pan.

5 While the chicken is cooking, melt the butter for the pilau in a large saucepan, add the onions and sauté on medium heat, stirring frequently, until dark brown. This will take about 20 minutes.

6 Drain and rinse the rice, then tip into the pan and stir to mix with the onions. Add the spices, bay leaves and salt and pour in about 900ml cold water to cover the rice. Stir and bring to the boil, turn the heat down to low and cover the pan. Simmer for 15 minutes without lifting the lid, then turn off the heat and leave until ready to serve.

7 When the curry is ready, remove the pan from the heat and sprinkle the top with the garam masala and coriander, plus the tomato and chillies if you like. Leave to stand for 5 minutes before serving with the rice.

January Jone-Omotajo

stuffed poussins with macaroni & cheese

4 poussins
8 sticks celery
125ml hot chicken stock
3 tbsp apricot preserve
1 tsp Dijon mustard

FOR THE STUFFING
85g cornbread stuffing mix (available
   in shops selling American ingredients)
   or your favourite packet stuffing mix
120ml boiling water
2 tbsp mild olive oil
1 onion, finely chopped
1 stick celery, finely chopped
1 green pepper, cored, deseeded and finely
   chopped
2 tsp Bell's seasoning
300g minced turkey

FOR THE MACARONI AND CHEESE
130g macaroni
40g Red Leicester cheese, grated
40g mature Cheddar cheese, grated
1 large egg, beaten
125ml whole milk
40g mild Cheddar cheese, grated
40g medium Cheddar cheese, grated
15g Parmesan cheese, grated
½ tsp paprika
25g butter

SERVES FOUR
This is not an everyday meal, but once your guests taste the succulent poussin with the mouth-watering stuffing, they will surely appreciate all your hard work. Bell's seasoning is an American brand of mixed herbs and spice – if you can't get it, use ½ tsp each dried rosemary, sage, oregano and marjoram with ¼ tsp ground ginger.

1 Prepare the stuffing for the poussins. Put the stuffing mix into a large bowl, pour in the boiling water and stir well to combine. Heat the olive oil in a frying pan on medium heat until hot. Add the onion, celery and green pepper and sauté until softened, about 5 minutes. Add the seasoning and turkey and cook for 10 minutes until the turkey is browned. Combine with the stuffing and allow to cool.

2 Preheat the oven to 180°C/Gas 4.

3 Season the cavities of the poussins and stuff with the turkey mixture. Place each poussin on top of 2 celery sticks in a roasting tray and pour the hot stock over the celery. Cover with foil and roast for 30 minutes.

4 Cook the macaroni in boiling salted water according to packet instructions. Drain well and place in a large bowl with the Red Leicester, mature Cheddar, egg and milk. Mix well, then layer with the mild and medium Cheddars in a 650ml ovenproof dish. Sprinkle with the Parmesan, paprika and black pepper to taste, and dot with the butter.

5 After the poussins have been cooking for 30 minutes, take them out of the oven and increase the temperature to 200°C/Gas 6. Gently heat the apricot preserve and mustard in a pan until melted to a glaze. Uncover the poussins and brush liberally with the glaze, then return them to the oven and roast uncovered for a further 25 minutes. Cover the breasts with foil if they get too brown.

6 When the birds have been roasting at the higher temperature for 15 minutes, put the macaroni in the oven and bake for 20 minutes until golden and bubbling.

7 At the end of the roasting time for the poussins, test by pushing a skewer between one of the thighs and the body – the juices should run clear. The stuffing should also be piping hot – 73°C at the centre. Leave the birds to rest in a warm place for 5–10 minutes before serving with the macaroni and cheese.

Harinder Khela

malai methi paneer & quorn curry

MALAI METHI PANEER
7.5cm piece fresh root ginger, chopped
6 cloves garlic, chopped
150ml boiling water
2 tbsp vegetable oil or butter
2 onions, chopped
2 tsp dried fenugreek leaves
1 tsp cumin seeds
1 tsp chilli powder (mild, medium or hot according to taste)
1 tsp turmeric
1 tsp garam masala
½–1 tsp salt
425g paneer (an Indian cheese), cut into cubes
single cream, to serve

QUORN CURRY
1 tbsp vegetable oil or butter
6cm piece fresh root ginger, finely chopped
5–6 cloves garlic, chopped
1 tsp dried fenugreek leaves
½ tsp cumin seeds
1 tsp Kitchen King (an Indian blend of spices – optional)
1 tsp garam masala
½ tsp salt
2 ripe tomatoes, chopped
200g peas (fresh or frozen)
1 tsp hot curry paste
375ml boiling water
1 x 300g pack Quorn mince

SERVES FOUR

No Indian meal would be complete without a cheese-based dish, and *malai methi paneer* is the genuine article. I can vouch for its authenticity – it came (with a few of my own adaptations) from one of the top cookery schools in India. The delicate flavour here is the fenugreek, which (as well as having a great taste) is claimed to increase potency as well as curing a million and one ailments. If you don't like a curry with too much sauce, this could be the one for you.

Malai methi paneer

1 Soak the ginger and garlic in the boiling water. Meanwhile, heat the oil or butter in a non-stick flameproof casserole or saucepan until hot. Add the onions and fry on low to medium heat until soft and translucent, 5–8 minutes. Add the fenugreek, cumin and ground spices with salt to taste, stir well and continue frying for a few minutes.

2 Drain the ginger and garlic water into the pan (discarding the ginger and garlic) and simmer very briefly until the water reduces a little. Now add the paneer and heat through on low heat for 5 minutes. Serve hot, moistened with cream to taste.

Quorn curry

1 Heat the oil or butter in a large, deep frying pan until hot. Add the ginger, garlic, fenugreek, cumin, ground spices and salt and fry on low to medium heat for 2–3 minutes, stirring constantly, until the ginger has softened.

2 Add the tomatoes and stir to mix, then fry for a few minutes until softened, stirring frequently.

3 Add the peas and cook for 4–5 minutes before stirring in the curry paste. Cook for a couple more minutes, pour in the boiling water and stir well.

4 Add the Quorn and simmer gently for 10 minutes, stirring frequently until the liquid is absorbed slightly and the flavours have had time to blend together. Leave to stand for 5 minutes before serving.

Dane Bowers

fillet of beef with port & redcurrant jus & garlic roast potatoes

1kg fillet of beef, tied with string
olive oil

FOR THE JUS
100ml port
100ml beef stock
2 tsp redcurrant jelly
olive oil
3 rashers bacon, finely chopped

FOR THE POTATOES
900g floury potatoes (such as Maris Piper
    or King Edward), peeled and cut into
    small cubes
2 cloves garlic, crushed
2 tsp chopped fresh rosemary
large knob of butter, softened
2 tbsp olive oil

SERVES FOUR
More than anything, I'm really into sauces and gravies. I made this dish because it had a posh-sounding one – redcurrant 'jus' just sounds fancy! I think that's what makes this meal so tasty. The cut of meat is also great as there is no fat, making this one of the tastiest beef dishes I've ever had. Oh, and don't kiss anyone after the garlic roast potatoes – I use loads!

1 Preheat the oven to 200°C/Gas 6.

2 Put the potatoes into a large saucepan of cold salted water, cover and bring to the boil on high heat. Lower the heat to medium and parboil the potatoes for 5 minutes. Drain and set aside. Mix the garlic and rosemary with the butter in a small bowl and set aside.

3 Put 2 tbsp olive oil into a roasting tin, place in the oven and heat until hot. Add the potatoes and turn to coat in the oil, then place in the oven and roast for 40 minutes, turning them over halfway through.

4 Meanwhile, season the beef with salt and pepper. Heat a splash of olive oil in a frying pan until very hot and sear the beef until browned on all sides. Transfer to another roasting tin and place in the oven with the potatoes. Roast for 20 minutes for rare meat, 25 minutes for medium-rare.

5 Make the jus while the meat and potatoes are roasting. Heat the port, stock and redcurrant jelly in a saucepan, stirring on low heat until the jelly has melted. Increase the heat and boil for 10–12 minutes or until reduced to 4–6 tbsp, stirring often. At the same time, heat a little olive oil in a frying pan and fry the bacon until crisp. Drain the bacon on kitchen paper, add to the jus and remove from the heat.

6 When the meat is done to your liking, take it out of the roasting tin and leave it to rest in a warm place for 10 minutes. Add the garlic butter to the potatoes and stir well, then roast for a further 5–10 minutes.

7 Pour the jus into the meat roasting tin on top of the stove and stir to scrape up any sediment and juices from the bottom of the tin. Slice the beef and serve at once, with the jus drizzled over and the roast potatoes on the side.

Richard Carpenter
rack of lamb with parsnip, potato & spinach gratin

olive oil
4 ripe large tomatoes, halved
1 aubergine, cut into 8 slices
2 French-trimmed racks of lamb, with
   6–7 ribs each

FOR THE GRATIN
knob of butter
1 onion, chopped or thinly sliced
400g parsnips, peeled and cut into
   1cm-thick slices
400g floury potatoes (such as Maris Piper
   or King Edward), peeled and cut into
   5mm-thick slices
400ml milk
300ml double cream
whole nutmeg
150g young spinach leaves

FOR THE DRESSING
3 tbsp extra virgin olive oil
1 tbsp red wine vinegar
1 tbsp chopped fresh mint

SERVES FIVE

This is an easy main course that can be left to cook while you and your guests eat the starter. The smell of the lamb roasting will have all your guests salivating. You could also cut the racks into individual portions so that your friends can pick them up and eat them with their fingers.

1 Prepare the gratin. Melt the butter in a shallow flameproof casserole until foaming and fry the onion on low heat until soft and translucent, 5–8 minutes. Add the parsnips, potatoes, milk and cream, then grate in nutmeg and add seasoning to taste. Cover the pan and simmer gently for 15 minutes or until the vegetables are just tender.

2 Remove the pan from the heat and add the spinach leaves a handful at a time, stirring them in gently and waiting for them to wilt before adding more. You can leave the gratin at this stage for several hours before baking. (Cover with foil and keep in the fridge if leaving for more than an hour.)

3 Preheat the oven to 200°C/Gas 6.

4 Heat a splash of olive oil in a large frying pan until hot and fry the cut sides of the tomato halves on medium to high heat for a few minutes until they are just coloured. Transfer to a roasting tray. Heat a little more olive oil in the pan and fry the aubergine slices until just coloured. It's best to work in 2 batches, and you may need to add more oil. Place in the roasting tray with the tomatoes.

5 Put the gratin in the oven and bake for 45 minutes.

6 Meanwhile, season the racks of lamb and sear in the hot frying pan until browned on all sides. Transfer to the tray with the vegetables and place in the oven next to the gratin. Roast for 20–25 minutes for rare to medium-rare meat, 30 minutes for medium. When the lamb is done to your liking, remove it from the tray and leave to rest in a warm place for 5 minutes, leaving the vegetables and gratin in the oven.

7 Make the dressing by whisking the ingredients together in a small bowl with salt and pepper to taste.

8 Carve the lamb between the bones and place on 5 warmed plates. Drizzle the meat with the dressing and serve the aubergines, tomatoes and gratin alongside.

desserts

Amit Koshal

chocolate samosas

200g Belgian chocolate, broken into
    small pieces
2 tbsp double cream
50g butter
4 sheets filo pastry (Jus-Rol is a good size
    for this recipe)

TO SERVE
4–6 scoops vanilla ice cream
2 tbsp chopped pistachio nuts

SERVES FOUR TO SIX

OK, so your guests have enjoyed a wonderful meal and are debating whether there is room for dessert. Now for my *pièce de résistance*. This twist on an Indian favourite will impress adults and children alike with your creativity. You may find it easier to practise making an unfilled samosa with some of the pastry you don't use before you attempt a filled one. But just see how easy they are to make!

1 Put the chocolate and cream into a bowl set over a pan of gently simmering water and heat gently until the chocolate has melted, stirring occasionally. Take the bowl off the pan and leave the chocolate to cool to room temperature. Melt the butter in a separate small pan.

2 Preheat the oven to 190°C/Gas 5.

3 Cut the pastry into 12 x 8cm-wide strips. Lay one strip horizontally in front of you and brush with melted butter. Take the bottom left-hand corner and fold up so that the short side edge is even with the top edge to make a triangle shape. Take the top left-hand corner and bring it down to the bottom edge so that the fold is even with the bottom edge and you have formed a triangular pocket.

4 Push a generous teaspoon of melted chocolate and cream into the pocket. Take the long flap and fold over at the top to enclose the chocolate. Keep diagonally folding and sticking down the buttery pastry, retaining the triangular shape until the pastry is used up. Stick down the end and coat with butter. Repeat to make 12 samosas in total.

5 Place the filled samosas on a baking sheet and brush with more melted butter. Bake for 8–10 minutes until light golden. Serve hot, with scoops of vanilla ice cream topped with pistachios.

Kelly Hatt

lime & tequila crème with chocolate-dipped ginger biscuits

300ml double cream
75g caster sugar
juice of 2–3 limes
1 tbsp gold tequila, or to taste

FOR THE GINGER BISCUITS
110g plain flour
1 tsp bicarbonate of soda
½ tsp ground ginger
pinch of ground cinnamon
pinch of salt
25g unsalted butter
50g soft brown sugar
50g golden syrup
2 tsp evaporated milk
80g dark chocolate (70% cocoa solids),
    broken into small pieces

SERVES FOUR

This is a classic lemon posset brought up to date with modern flavours. Lime and tequila work really well together, and the crunchy texture and bitterness of the biscuits make them the perfect accompaniment.

1 Put the cream and sugar into a saucepan. Bring slowly to the boil, stirring to dissolve the sugar, then simmer for 3 minutes, stirring all the time.

2 Remove the pan from the heat. Pour in the juice of 2 limes, stirring to combine – the cream should start to thicken instantly. Now stir in 1 tbsp tequila and taste the crème. Add a little more lime juice if the flavour is not tart enough, plus more tequila if you want.

3 Pour the crème into 4 x 125ml glasses and cover with clingfilm. Chill in the fridge for at least 6 hours, ideally overnight.

4 Make the biscuits. Sift the flour, soda, spices and salt into a bowl. Melt the butter, sugar and syrup in a pan, leave to cool slightly, then mix into the dry ingredients with the evaporated milk to make a dough. Wrap in clingfilm and chill in the fridge for at least 30 minutes.

5 Preheat the oven to 180°C/Gas 4. Butter a large baking tray.

6 Roll out the dough on a lightly floured surface to about 5mm thick and cut into 10 fingers, discs or any other shape you fancy. I prefer fingers as they are easier to dip into the chocolate later, and they are also a good shape for dipping into the crème.

7 Place the biscuits on the baking tray and bake for 8–10 minutes until golden brown. Remove from the oven and leave to cool for a couple of minutes on the tray, then transfer to a wire rack to cool completely.

8 Melt the chocolate in a heatproof bowl set over a pan of gently simmering water. Remove the bowl from the pan and dip in the biscuits one at a time, coating about half of each biscuit. Place the biscuits on non-stick baking parchment to set.

9 Serve the crème straight from the fridge, with the biscuits for dipping.

Alastair James

al's limoncello tart with homemade vanilla ice cream

FOR THE ICE CREAM
3 large egg yolks
250ml whipping cream
40g caster sugar
seeds from ½ vanilla pod
1 tsp vanilla extract

FOR THE PASTRY
175g plain flour
pinch of salt
85g chilled unsalted butter,
    cut into small cubes
1 large egg, separated
2–4 tbsp cold water

FOR THE FILLING
50g unsalted butter, softened
125g caster sugar
50g ground almonds
2 large eggs
1 large egg yolk
finely grated zest and juice of
    2 unwaxed lemons
125ml double cream
100ml limoncello liqueur

TO SERVE
250g raspberries
1 tbsp icing sugar, sifted

SERVES SIX

This is a great twist on a dessert that everyone loves and that goes with just about any kind of meal. Make sure you're not too shy with the limoncello! A minute on the lips, a lifetime on the hips – but this is totally worth it. (Be warned that this homemade vanilla ice cream contains raw eggs.)

1 Make the ice cream. Beat all the ingredients in a bowl with an electric mixer until the beaters leave a ribbon trail when lifted. Spoon the mixture into a rigid container, cover and freeze for at least 6 hours until firm. (If you have an ice-cream maker, churn until thick, then freeze.)

2 Make the pastry. Sift the flour and salt into a large bowl. Drop in the cubes of butter and rub them into the flour until the mixture looks like breadcrumbs. Add the egg yolk and stir in with enough cold water to make a smooth dough. Wrap in clingfilm and chill in the fridge for 30 minutes.

3 Remove the clingfilm and roll the dough out on a lightly floured surface until about 3mm thick. Use to line a 20cm loose-bottomed tart tin that is about 3.5cm deep. Prick the pastry on the bottom with a fork and chill for 10 minutes.

4 Preheat the oven to 190°C/Gas 5.

5 Line the tart with greaseproof paper or foil and fill with baking beans, then bake blind for 15 minutes until the pastry has set. Remove the paper and beans and paint the inside of the tart with the egg white to seal the pastry. Bake for a further 5 minutes. Remove from the oven and turn the heat down to 150°C/Gas 2.

5 Make the filling. Beat the butter and sugar by hand or with an electric mixer; stir in the almonds. Beat the eggs and egg yolk in a bowl, add the remaining ingredients, then blend into the butter mixture until smooth.

7 Pour the filling into the pastry case and bake for 40 minutes until nearly set. Increase the heat to 180°C/Gas 4 and bake for another 10 minutes until golden brown.

8 Allow the tart to cool for about 15 minutes. At the same time, remove the ice cream from the freezer to make it easier to scoop. Serve the tart with the raspberries and icing sugar and scoops of ice cream.

Ita Egan

banana & caramel crunch

1 x 397g can condensed milk
3 large bananas
275–300ml double cream
2 tbsp icing sugar
grated milk chocolate, to decorate

FOR THE BASE
150g digestive biscuits
75g butter

This is heaven for those with a sweet tooth! I got this recipe from an old head chef I knew (hi, Jeremy), and after a hard day in a busy kitchen, this pud was a just reward. Trust me – you will be amazed at how good this tastes. The combination of caramel, banana, biscuit and cream really works and is delicious. I always add a little icing sugar to my whipped cream as I feel it's a little bland without it. Enjoy!

1 Place the unopened can of condensed milk in a large, deep heavy saucepan and cover generously with water. Bring to the boil and boil gently for 3 hours, checking regularly that the can is fully submerged in water. After this time, carefully remove the can from the water and leave to cool completely before opening.

2 To make the base, place the biscuits in a plastic bag and crush into fine crumbs with a rolling pin. Melt the butter in a saucepan and mix with the crushed biscuits. Press over the bottom of a lightly oiled 20cm springform or loose-bottomed cake tin. Chill in the fridge for 30 minutes, or until firm.

3 Spoon the caramel from the can over the biscuit base. Peel the bananas, cut into 1.5cm-thick slices and arrange over the caramel.

4 Pour the cream into a bowl and sift in the icing sugar, then whip to soft peaks.

5 Remove the dessert from the cake tin and place on a serving plate. Spread or pipe the cream over the bananas and sprinkle grated chocolate on top. If not serving immediately, keep in the fridge without the grated chocolate – this should go on at the last moment.

Paul Condliffe

chocolate & orange liqueur terrine with raspberry sauce

vegetable oil, for greasing
150g good-quality dark chocolate, broken into small pieces
4 tbsp orange liqueur
175g butter, cut into small cubes
150g good-quality milk chocolate, broken into small pieces
1 x 284ml carton double cream, at room temperature

FOR THE RASPBERRY SAUCE
2 x 150g punnets raspberries
1 tbsp cornflour
125ml cold water
2 tbsp caster sugar

SERVES EIGHT TO TEN

Chocolate, cream, butter and liqueur – forget the diet for a week or maybe a month, we're only here once so let's enjoy ourselves! It's yummy and scrummy, and you can bet your guests will want a bit more.

1 Lightly grease a 22 x 12 x 6cm loaf tin and line with clingfilm, leaving a generous overhang.

2 Put the dark chocolate, liqueur and half the butter into a heatproof bowl. Set the bowl over a pan of gently simmering water and heat until the chocolate is melted and smooth, stirring occasionally. Remove the bowl from the pan, then melt the milk chocolate in another bowl with the remaining butter. Leave both bowls of chocolate to cool to room temperature.

3 Whip the cream until it is thick enough to hold its shape. Fold half the whipped cream into each bowl of chocolate until evenly mixed.

4 Spoon the dark chocolate into the prepared tin and smooth the surface. Chill in the fridge for 10–15 minutes to firm up slightly, then spoon the milk chocolate over the dark layer and smooth the surface. Cover the top of the terrine with the overhanging clingfilm and refrigerate for at least 2–3 hours (or overnight) until firm.

5 To make the raspberry sauce, whiz the fruit to a purée in a blender, then pass through a fine sieve into a small saucepan to remove the seeds. Put the cornflour into a small bowl and mix to a paste with a few spoonfuls of the measured water. Pour the remaining water into the purée in the pan, add the sugar and stir on low heat until the sugar has dissolved. Bring to the boil, then trickle in the cornflour paste, stirring constantly. Simmer, stirring, for a minute or so until the sauce thickens, then cool and refrigerate until ready to serve.

6 To serve, loosen the sides of the clingfilm away from the tin with a knife, then turn the terrine out on to a board and peel off the clingfilm. Cut into 8–10 slices and serve with the raspberry sauce.

Natasha Hamilton

lemon & lime cheesecake

FOR THE BASE
12 digestive biscuits
75g butter, cut into small cubes
1 tbsp runny honey

FOR THE FILLING
500g full-fat soft cheese, at room
    temperature
115g caster sugar
finely grated zest and juice of
    1 unwaxed lemon
finely grated zest and juice of
    1 unwaxed lime
150ml double cream
raspberries, to decorate

SERVES SIX TO EIGHT

Dessert should have the 'wow' factor, and that this is so simple to make allows you to reap the rewards without even breaking into a sweat! You can pack it with as much flavour as you want – if you want a strong citrus flavour then add more rind and juice, but take it slowly as it can split the cheese mixture. This is delicious served with a raspberry coulis, and is bound to be a highlight of your meal.

1 To make the base, place the biscuits in a plastic bag and crush into fine crumbs with a rolling pin. Melt the butter with the honey in a saucepan and mix with the crushed biscuits in a bowl. Press over the bottom of a lightly buttered 20cm springform or loose-bottomed cake tin. Set aside in the fridge while you make the filling.

2 Put the cheese into a bowl with the sugar and the lemon and lime zest. Pour in the lemon and lime juice and beat well.

3 Whip the cream in a bowl until it just holds a soft shape, then fold into cheese mixture until evenly blended.

4 Spoon the mixture into the tin and smooth over the top with a knife. Chill in the fridge until set, 1½–2 hours (or leave overnight). Unmould and decorate with raspberries before serving.

Daniel Bowman

praline liqueur cheesecake

FOR THE BASE
150g digestive biscuits
75g unsalted butter

FOR THE FILLING
finely grated zest and juice of
    1 unwaxed lemon
1 x 12g sachet gelatine powder
275–300ml double cream
2 medium egg whites
400g full-fat soft cheese, at room
    temperature
125ml praline liqueur
115g caster sugar
fresh mint sprigs, to decorate

SERVES SIX TO EIGHT

This luxurious cheesecake is really simple to make and is an indulgent end to a dinner party. To achieve the lightness of the cheesecake you must whisk the egg whites until they form stiff peaks and then fold into the cheese mixture, as described below. The gentle folding maintains the lightness. It can be made with any creamy liqueur and works exceptionally well with all the Baileys range and even Amarula. Ensure a good cup of liqueur is used and remember, don't eat and drive!

1 To make the base, place the biscuits in a plastic bag and crush into fine crumbs with a rolling pin. Melt the butter in a saucepan and mix with the crushed biscuits in a bowl. Press over the bottom of a lightly oiled 20cm springform or loose-bottomed cake tin. Chill in the fridge while preparing the filling.

2 Make the filling. Put the lemon juice into a small heatproof bowl, sprinkle over the gelatine and leave for a few minutes until spongy. Now stand the bowl in a pan of hot water and heat gently until the gelatine has dissolved, stirring occasionally. Remove the bowl from the pan.

3 Whip the cream in a bowl until soft peaks form. In a separate bowl, whisk the egg whites until they form stiff peaks.

4 Beat the cheese in a large bowl with the lemon zest, liqueur and sugar until smooth. Stir in the gelatine, then gently fold in the cream and egg whites until evenly incorporated.

5 Spoon the filling over the biscuit base and chill in the fridge for at least 3 hours or until set. Decorate with sprigs of mint before serving.

Bindi Holding

lemon & lime syllabub in brandy snap baskets with mulled strawberries

FOR THE SYLLABUB
finely grated zest and juice of
    1 unwaxed lemon
finely grated zest of ½ unwaxed lime
75g caster sugar
1 tbsp brandy
2 tbsp sweet sherry
275–300ml double cream
juice of ½ lime, or to taste

FOR THE MULLED STRAWBERRIES
200ml red wine
100ml water
50g caster sugar
1 cinnamon stick
½ tsp green peppercorns
1 x 3g sachet mulled wine spice
200g strawberries, hulled and halved
    or quartered depending on size

TO SERVE
6 brandy snap baskets
grated fresh coconut

SERVES SIX

Syllabub may be hard to spell, but the glory will be all yours when you whip up this relatively simple-to-make dessert. This one is all about velvety cream, tropical tang, lashings of brandy and a subtle but distinctive hint of pepper in your gorgeously poached strawberries. Warning: Do Not Burn the Coconut.

1 Make the syllabub. Soak the lemon and lime zest in the lemon juice for 2–3 hours.

2 Add the sugar, brandy and sherry to the lemon juice and stir well.

3 Whip the cream in a large bowl until it holds soft peaks. Fold in the lemon juice mixture, then add lime juice to taste. Cover the bowl and chill in the fridge for 2–3 hours to firm up (or leave overnight).

4 Prepare the syrup for the strawberries. Pour the red wine and water into a saucepan and add the sugar, cinnamon stick, peppercorns and the sachet of spice. Place the pan on low heat and stir until the sugar has dissolved, then increase the heat and boil until reduced and syrupy, about 10 minutes. Remove from the heat and strain into a bowl. Leave to cool.

5 Preheat the grill on medium setting and line a baking tray with foil. Sprinkle the coconut over the tray and place under the grill for a few minutes until golden brown. Watch carefully and turn the coconut over from time to time, to ensure even browning. Remove from the heat and leave to cool.

6 To serve, divide the syllabub between the brandy snap baskets. Add the strawberries to the syrup, spoon over the syllabub and sprinkle with toasted coconut. Serve straightaway or the baskets will not stay crisp.

Jodie Marsh

ginger & orange syrup cheesecakes

6 digestive biscuits
40g butter, plus extra for greasing
4–5 pieces stem ginger and 4 tbsp ginger
   syrup (from a jar)
½ x 298g can mandarin orange segments in
   natural juice, well drained
300g full-fat soft cheese, at room temperature
grated dark chocolate, to decorate

SERVES FOUR

These are the easiest things to make but they taste amazing! The mixture of the sweet, sticky syrup and the soft cheese makes for a taste of pure heaven, and the ginger makes them more sophisticated than any other fruity cheesecake. This dessert can be modified in many ways (you could use chocolate digestives for the base, for example). By decorating with grated chocolate and mandarin orange slices, they look impressive when served. This is a fine dessert for people who enjoy fine dining!

1 Stand 4 metal rings, each 9cm in diameter and 3cm tall, on a baking sheet. Brush inside the rings and the baking sheet with butter.

2 Place the biscuits in a plastic bag and crush into fine crumbs with a rolling pin. Melt the butter in a small saucepan and mix with the crushed biscuits in a bowl. Divide the mixture equally between the buttered rings and press down firmly to form the base of each cheesecake.

3 Cut 8 thin slivers from a piece of stem ginger and set aside. Finely dice the remaining ginger. Reserve 4 whole mandarin segments and chop the rest.

4 Put the diced ginger into a bowl with the 4 tbsp ginger syrup and the cheese. Beat until soft and smooth, then add the chopped mandarins and mix everything together gently but thoroughly.

5 Divide the mixture between the rings and level the tops with a knife. Cover and refrigerate until firm, 1½–2 hours (they can be left overnight).

6 To serve, transfer the cheesecakes to 4 plates and carefully remove the rings. Decorate the top of each cheesecake with 2 of the reserved stem ginger slices, 1 mandarin segment and some grated chocolate.

Gill Buley

profiteroles with hot chocolate sauce

FOR THE CHOUX PASTRY
60g butter, cut into small cubes, plus extra
   for greasing
150ml water
75g plain flour, sifted
2 medium eggs, beaten

FOR THE CHOCOLATE SAUCE
175g dark chocolate, broken into small pieces
300ml cold water
115g granulated sugar

TO SERVE
300ml double or whipping cream
1 x 150g punnet raspberries
fresh mint sprigs

SERVES FIVE

A week before my *Come Dine With Me* dinner party I took my first ever choux pastry lesson with my dad's wife, Lesley. She pulled out a very old and tatty piece of paper, her well-used and reliable recipe for profiteroles. I got to work and it really was easy, although you need a lot of arm muscle. The results are worth it though – a huge mountain of profiteroles, nicely garnished with fresh raspberries and a few sprigs of mint, is the ultimate showstopper.

1 Preheat the oven to 200°C/Gas 6. Butter a large baking sheet.

2 Make the choux pastry. Melt the butter in a medium saucepan with the water, then bring rapidly to the boil. Remove the pan from the heat and shoot in the flour, then stir and beat vigorously until a smooth paste is formed (a few seconds). Add the beaten eggs a little at a time, beating hard after each addition, then continue beating until the paste looks glossy.

3 Dampen the buttered baking sheet by sprinkling with water. Put the choux paste into a large piping bag fitted with a large plain nozzle and pipe 15 buns on to the sheet. Bake for 10 minutes, then increase the oven temperature to 220°C/Gas 7 and bake for a further 10–15 minutes, until the profiteroles are crisp. Remove the profiteroles to a wire rack and make a small slit in the bottom of each one to let the steam escape. Leave to cool.

4 For the chocolate sauce, put the chocolate into a pan, pour in the water and place on low heat until the chocolate has melted and is smooth, stirring frequently. Add the sugar and stir until dissolved, then bring to the boil and simmer for 10–15 minutes, stirring occasionally, until the sauce has a syrupy, coating consistency. Remove from the heat and keep warm.

5 Whip the cream in a bowl until it holds its shape and place in a clean piping bag fitted with a plain nozzle. Enlarge the slit in the profiteroles (or cut them in half) and fill with cream.

6 To serve, pile the profiteroles on a plate and decorate with raspberries and mint. Pour the sauce over the profiteroles as you serve them to your guests.

entertaining throughout the year

Entertaining isn't just about the big dates throughout the year – Christmas, New Year's Eve or Easter. There are lots of other reasons for having a party at any time – everything from anniversary celebrations to coming up with a theme as an excuse for a party, simply because you haven't seen your mates for a while. And more people than ever are staging their own *Come Dine With Me* competitions, so here are a few tips on staging parties which can slot into your diary at any time from 1 January to the end of December.

anniversary entertaining

When it comes to celebrating your parents' or in-laws' wedding anniversary, think about what the couple in question would like. If they're marking a special anniversary they might not want a house full of people, instead preferring a smaller get-together with close family. There are three different couples to take into account: the 'no expense spared, we know what we want' brigade; the 'we're determined to do something, but are slightly dreading the organization/don't know what to do' types; and the 'we don't want a fuss' people.

If your parents or in-laws fall into the first category then you could be laughing, as they'll be determined to do it all themselves. Alternatively, they could have all the ideas (and the dosh) but delegate the organization to you, so that it's your job to book the venue and the caterers, draw up the guest list, choose the music, etc. In that case, just bombard them with questions to make sure they get what they want, and sort it out for them.

If your relatives fall into category two – determined to celebrate somehow, but slightly dreading it or don't know what to do – then things aren't too bad either. All you need to do is encourage them to think about what they want in good time. If they can't decide then simply lock

them in a room and don't let them out until they've made up their minds. Once they've decided, it's a matter of badgering them for a guest list and food and drink suggestions, and going ahead with the arrangements (see below).

The real work piles up if the guests of honour fall into category three. These are the modest parents or in-laws who don't like to make a fuss about themselves, but secretly would be chuffed to bits if someone else did. Perhaps they'd never say so to anyone, perhaps not even to their spouse, because it would all be a bit too forward, too brash, too OTT. Don't take their word for it. Instead organize a surprise do for them. They'll love it.

If your parents or in-laws aren't the restaurant types, or you're worried that some guests won't want to eat out, then why not cater for a party yourself? If you've been to all that trouble it will make the guests of honour appreciate the day even more. But as with any party, you need to do your research: here are a few things you need to look into.

Who to invite: Close family come top of the guest list. In all likelihood, the couple will be happy to be surrounded with their children and grandchildren: most of us nowadays struggle to spend enough time with our families. Make sure that everyone knows the relevant anniversary date, and if there are lots of sons and grandsons in the family then they've probably forgotten, so get it into their diaries early and issue reminders. Ensure they keep a couple of other weekends free on either side, too (see below).

After that it's a question of working out which uncles and aunts your parents or in-laws get on with (don't assume it's all of them). This is the hardest part of your research, to discover who should be invited and who your parents would really rather not see. If in doubt invite them all, and work out which ones need to be steered away from the booze because they can't be trusted around free alcohol.

After that, subtly check who their best friends are. One good pointer if you're married is to invite anyone your parents (or in-laws) insisted should come to your wedding – if they were at your nuptials, then that means they're good mates with your parents. Do this even if it means inviting the guy who insisted on one too many dances with the bridesmaids.

Don't forget, your parents' friends will move in self-contained circles, so make sure everyone is invited, otherwise some will be mortally offended. Once you start inviting people, check the guest list with them. Be careful not to take just one person's word for it, though – they might be the stirrer of the group who thinks it'll be funny if your mum has to share a drink with the bowling club member she no longer speaks to after a scoring dispute in the final last year.

Instead, ask the same question to a few people. Once the same names crop up, you're probably safe (unless all your parents' friends are practical jokers with the same sense of humour). Hopefully that way you'll secure everyone your parents would want to be there.

Which date: The next thing is to work out a suitable date. If the soon-to-be-celebrating husband is an old smoothie, he'll have organized something for the actual date of their wedding anniversary. And if he hasn't, it's incumbent on you as their child to ensure that he does, pronto, to ensure there are no scenes.

That means the date of the anniversary itself should be out of the running for the celebrations, so the next best date will be any Saturday or Sunday for at least two or three weeks after that – you need to keep enough dates open just in case your dad decides it's time to finally go on that two-week cruise that he's been talking about for years. That's the reason why you need the rest of your family to block out lots of potential dates.

The venue: This is the trickiest problem of all. If they are the 'we don't want a fuss' types, they won't know the party's happening at all so it'll be harder to host it at their house, but not impossible. Use the same tricks you would for Mother's Day to get them out while you set up. If their home doesn't give you enough space then use a family member's bigger house, if it's near enough. If you have no luck then try to find a cheap village hall or similar.

What sort of party: Think about the people for whom you're hosting the party. It's not for you – it's for your parents or parents-in-law – and they probably have very different tastes. They think a vodka luge is a sport in the Winter Olympics and a snakebite is what you get in the Australian Outback, so pitch it right.

Food: If you've got a lot of people coming, the best option is probably a buffet – it allows people to mingle, and is also a lot less fuss to organize. Plus you can also spread the pain of cooking for that number of people among the rest of the family.

Think about what cooking facilities you have: there's no point in everyone bringing lasagnes, pies and other hot dishes if there's only one small oven which will quickly be overloaded with food. If everything has to go into the oven then everyone will still get to eat, but only hours after they have arrived. By this time they'll probably be thoroughly plastered, and the chances are your embarrassing uncle will decide to tell cringe-worthy stories about your dad's previous girlfriends.

Instead, opt for hot and cold options: pies and bakes alongside pre-cooked quiches, cold salmon, etc. Choose vegetable dishes that can be done on the hob, or salads even, rather than lots of roasted side dishes that will take up valuable oven space. To make life easier, opt for cold puddings or a cheese board.

Choose dishes which can be prepared in advance: when you get to the party you'll have so much else to do – putting out plates, pouring drinks, greeting guests – that you won't want to be peeling spuds, chopping carrots or washing lettuce.

Pudding: If you're feeling really brave, you could go for a very special pudding: a reproduction of the wedding cake from their big day. That'll need some serious planning, but it will be a nice touch that will bring back good memories.

Drink: As with any party, do sale or return and get the glasses chucked in too. Check your parents' wine cellar to see what they're drinking and order that, plus some beer, and perhaps also offer a simple mixer option like gin and tonic.

Serving: If you can afford it, one thing worth clubbing together for is someone to oversee the booze. You'll need a good barman or woman from the local pub who can make sure that people's drinks are topped up, that there's enough cold beer in the fridge and that Uncle Richard doesn't hog the champagne bottle. If you can't afford that option then make a rota among the key family members, taking turns to do the job for an hour each; that way you can all mingle for a while, but also ensure that people are being properly served.

Music: Make an effort and dig out stuff that brings back happy memories for your parents: wedding songs, music they listened to when they met, hits from when the kids were born. Raid their music collection, pretending you've suddenly developed an interest in 1970s pop, or ask their friends. That way you can compile a good play list in advance

and just stick the MP3 player on a speaker system and let it burble on all afternoon without a second thought.

A trip down memory lane: Don't be afraid to help them get all nostalgic: dig out photos – of their wedding, other anniversaries, particularly memorable holidays, their children's births – and compile an album for them and their guests to flick through. If you're feeling really organized, you could even try to put a slide-show together, or play any movie film you might have.

A speech: Work out who's the best speaker in the family and get them to say a few words. If you're all a bit bashful when it comes to public speaking then pair up so that you can share the pain! And if even that is a bit daunting, throw in a few visual aids to help out. You could get some recorded messages to play during the speech – this is a nice touch if people can't be there for the day itself.

Guest book: It shouldn't just be for weddings: get the guests to write something as a tribute to the couple. Also appoint someone as official photographer to get some nice photos – perhaps a good job for the grandkids. You could even get them to wheel out a video camera, for a video guest book.

With that all in place, you should have the perfect day for your parents or in-laws.

themed dinners, unusual party tricks and pets

Once you reckon you're a dab hand at dinner parties you'll be itching to spice things up. Throwing a themed evening is one obvious way to make a dinner with a regular group of friends feel a bit different. But beware – it can often be the downfall of even the best host, as many *Come Dine With Me* contestants have discovered to their cost.

Here are a few tips on what to do, and what not to do, for a themed night.

- Make the theme crystal clear or risk leaving your diners red-faced with embarrassment, as Taunton host Richard Smith discovered. He threw a Waterloo night and wanted everyone to dress accordingly. He thought it would be obvious he was talking about the battle that saw Napoleon's final downfall, but guest Paula McShane wasn't a history boffin and thought he was a fan of Abba's Eurovision hit. She was left feeling rather out of it with her seventies-style fancy dress.

- Not everyone will necessarily share your passions, so test out your ideas on your friends first. If you get a so-so reaction then you know it's not for everyone. For instance, take nurse Andie Todd, who thought it would be a great idea to get her guests to hold her chickens. They didn't want to (I can't think why) and she never really managed to recover from that moment, ending up fifth … out of five.

- If you are going to do something wacky, it helps if everyone can laugh about it. Ian Jones in Dudley spiced up his evening with some sausage-making. It helped break the ice, leaving the diners in hysterics, and also gave them something to take home and fry up for breakfast the next day. It all helped Ian to reach a winning score.

- Think about getting some help. To avoid over-burdening yourself with the theme, don't be afraid to get some mates to give you a helping hand. To make it really work, choose a theme that you can plan in advance. Jane Bates from Manchester did exactly that – she laid on a Hollywood-themed night complete with red carpet, Oscar-style statues and fake paparazzi. Her mates pretended to be photographers so that when the guests turned up dressed as their favourite film stars, they were papped by the fake snappers. The extra help – and that clever forward-planning – meant that Jane could concentrate on her food during the evening, helping her bag that £1,000 winner's prize.

- Fancy dress is not best done alone. City boy Ryan Waters decided to do a caveman evening, which included dressing himself in a caveman-style fake animal skin. He looked rather out of place, though, as he hadn't asked his guests to dress up too.

- Think about who's coming to dinner, and tailor your entertainment accordingly. Claire Baron from York thought it would be a great idea to give her evening a Mexican feel, so she handed out hats and fake moustaches. Perhaps unsurprisingly it wasn't a hit with all of her guests, with one, Famida Wilson, being particularly unimpressed with her false facial hair. Claire then compounded the problem when she asked everyone to play a game which involved trying to bash a model donkey hanging from a tree to get all the sweets out – known as a *piñata* – but Famida wasn't a fan of that either.

- Be careful with the booze: a themed night is great but don't get carried away with the drink. Claire Monahan threw a West Country themed party in north Somerset, with all her locally sourced food washed down by local cider, followed by more cider. It was very strong and left one contestant, David Elsmore, rather worse for wear as the night progressed. Claire's food may not have been appreciated as much as she may have hoped and she missed out on the £1,000 prize.

- Don't allow your pets to enter the dining room. Ever. Claire Baron from York got her pet snake out during pudding, only for it to leave a rather unpleasant deposit on the table. Unsurprisingly, no one wanted dessert.

- Make sure your theme doesn't get taken the wrong way. Hairdresser Jay Davies from Stoke thought it would be a good idea to throw a wig party. But when guest Caroline Hicky turned up wearing a wig completely different from her normal look, bookie Linda Jackson told Caroline that it seemed more natural than her real hair. To make matters worse fellow guest Paul Condliffe weighed in, saying she looked about five stone slimmer. On top of all that, Linda donned a large blonde wig, claiming she wanted to look like Caroline. They all thought they were being nice, but Caroline was rather peeved and the next night told the others just how upset she'd been.

- If you're planning party games, think them through carefully. Bindi Holding from London decided to get her guests to play a game that involved picking up a cardboard box with their teeth. The box was cut smaller each time someone picked it up, which meant that the players had to bend over more and more. Bindi hadn't reckoned on the short dress worn by guest Nicole Ganz, so by the time the box was not much taller than a matchbox, Nicole found herself in some rather exposed positions.

- After-dinner dancing isn't always a winner. It can add atmosphere to your evening, but only if your guests share your passion for it, otherwise you're in trouble. Audrey Gordon from Manchester thought the perfect dinner party ended with a dance, but she found herself boogieing on her own in her dining room.

- Don't do too much. Wearing fancy dress, donning hats and playing games can be fun, but doing all of them at the same time can be a bit too much forced revelry for one night. It can also mean that you end up taking your mind off the food which is, after all, the main reason why people are coming to dinner. Exactly that happened to catering manager Kellan Dalton at her party in Derby. She threw a Japanese-themed night, complete with kimonos and headgear for the guests to wear, then got them to dress up in sumo wrestling outfits to

try sumo wrestling. But with so much to think about – including three courses of complicated Japanese nosh – she admitted at the end of the night that her party didn't work as well as she'd hoped. Not surprisingly, she didn't win.

- Don't give your wilder guests the chance to take advantage of your theme or food, as Michael Barrymore's rivals discovered to their cost in the celebrity game-show hosts special. On Pat Sharpe's night, Barrymore took the Greek theme to extremes by smashing his main-course plate on the floor, but that was topped on the third night when Jenny Powell's creamy Eton mess became a custard pie that ended up in Jenny and Anthea Redfern's faces.

- Beware of taking a theme too far. A sushi night is fun, but possibly not when the sushi is served up on a near-naked teenager, as hairdresser Craig Lockett did in Bristol. He roped in a friend to lie on his table, dressed only in his boxer shorts, with the sushi served on his unwaxed stomach. Funnily enough his guests didn't approve and he ended up last.

- Be careful with presents. Alicia Coppola from Manchester thought she'd provide some drawings for her guests to take home with them, only for diner Bessie Hilton to say that hers made her look ugly and like something out of a horror movie. Luckily Alicia's food made up for her poorly received artwork and she went on to win the competition.

- Remember the age of your diners. Brighton host Ana Jalley thought it would be fun to stage a dance involving two teddy bears, in homage to a teddy bears' picnic. Unfortunately her guests were adults so they didn't quite get it, leaving Ana empty-handed when the winner was announced.

- Avoid practical jokes. They might sound like a good idea, but remember that your idea of funny might be someone else's idea of gross. Surveyor Dave Wheeler decided his guests would be game for a laugh, so he left fake poo for them to find on their tour of the house and put a fart machine under his dinner table, remotely operating it from the kitchen. Not everyone shared Dave's toilet humour and he finished in last place but one.

• Beware of leaving flamboyant clothes lying around, as you never know who'll slip into them. Nail technician trainer Caroline Hicky left one of her elaborate evening gowns on a hanger outside her wardrobe, only for guest Paul Condliffe to take such a shine to it that he came down during dessert dressed in it. Luckily, she took it all in good heart.

• Finally, don't let your theme or entertainment distract your own attention from the food. In north London, Timothy Sanderson spent so much time enjoying the burlesque dancing he'd laid on that it slipped his mind to check on his ice cream, leaving it rock solid and almost impossible to serve.

how to organize your own *come dine with me*

Organizing your own *Come Dine With Me* competition is now all the rage, so here's how to do it.

Participants: It's best to arrange one with friends. By all means place an ad on the internet asking for like-minded people to take part, but don't blame me if you get lumbered with a load of weirdos.

Budget: To ensure a level playing field, decide how much people can spend and keep it reasonable – not everyone's a moneybags!

Dates: The show is filmed over consecutive nights but that's a tall order, so agree on dates which are spread over a few weeks for your dinner parties.

Order: Decide this by pulling names out of a hat.

Menus: To ensure that no one gains an unfair advantage by tweaking their dinner after seeing everyone else's efforts, all menus should be submitted in advance. It helps if you can find someone who's impartial – perhaps a friend who can't make all the dates.

Themes: You could go the whole hog and do themed nights, but again this must be submitted in advance. And of course, beware of the pitfalls outlined above!

Prize: Get everyone to chip in equally for a cash prize, or agree on something like a meal out for the winner.

Scoring: To ensure fairness, keep it secret. After each dinner, guests should write their scores down and seal them in an envelope (along with comments!). To prevent skulduggery, everyone should sign the sealed envelope so it's clear that no one has seen anyone else's scores.

Results: Enrol a spouse or friend of the final host to count the scores on the last evening, then let the drum roll as they reveal who's won ... and who's come last. They could even read out some comments as well, either anonymously or, if you're all feeling brave, revealing who they've come from.

Show the world: Take lots of pictures, then upload them to Channel 4's *Come Dine With Me* homepage at www.channel4.com/dine

index